YOUNG STUDENTS
Learning Library®

VOLUME 6

Color —
Denmark

NEWFIELD
PUBLICATIONS
SHELTON, CONNECTICUT

CREDITS

Page 644 Pat Morris; 648 ZEFA; 649 Colorado Dept. Pub. Relations; 652 Smithsonian Institute (top); Peter Newark (middle); 654 Robert Opie; 656 British Museum (top); Mary Evans (middle); Hulton (bottom); 657 Marconi Company Ltd. (top); Sony Ltd. (bottom); 660 ZEFA (top); J. Allan Cash (bottom); 662 Science Museum; 666 Feranti (top); IBM (bottom); 671 Girandon; 674 United States Capitol Historical Society; 677 ZEFA; 678 ZEFA (top); J. Allan Cash (bottom); 682 Armando Curcio Editore; 683 ZEFA; 684 National Gallery (bottom); 688 Armando Curcio Editore (top); ZEFA (bottom); 694 Library of Congress; 696 National Maritime Museum (top); 696 PhotoDisc, Inc. (bottom); 697 PhotoDisc, Inc. ZEFA (bottom); 700 the Bettmann Archive (bottom); 703 British Museum; 705 J. Allan Cash; 709 ZEFA; 710 Peter Newark Pictures; 711 United States Secret Service; 712 NYS Commerce Dept.; 713 Robert Harding; 715 Peter Newark Pictures; 717 C.R. Warne (top); 718 Jane Turomey; 719 Martyn Moxon; 723 Armando Curcio Editore; 724 National Portrait Gallery; 725 Armando Curcio Editore (top); 733 ZEFA; 734 Barnaby's Picture Library; 735 National Library of Medicine, Bethesda; 736 Peter Newark Pictures; 738 Armando Curcio Editore; 740 MOMO; 741 ZEFA; 742 Boulogne Chamber of Commerce; 743 ZEFA; 744 Editorial Photocolor Archives; 746 National Film Archives; 747 SATOUR; 748 SCALA; 751 United States Air Force Official Photograph (middle); Armando Curcio Editore (bottom); 753 Israel Government Tourist Office; 754 Armando Curcio Editore (top); ZEFA (middle); 756 Mike Grey; 757 Ron Boardman; 758 Armando Curcio Editore; 759 NHPA; 761 Armando Curcio Editore; 762 Armando Curcio Editore (top left); Tate Gallery (middle); Armando Curcio Editore (bottom); 763 Armando Curcio Editore (top); Delaware State Travel Services (bottom); 764 Delaware State Travel Services; 767 ZEFA.

Young Students Learning Library and Newfield Publications are federally registered trademarks of Newfield Publications, Inc.

Printed in the U.S.A.

ISBN 0-8374-9813-9

CONTENTS

▲ The California redwood is the world's tallest tree. It is a **CONIFER** and grows up to 370 feet (112 m) tall.

☀ COLOR

Light is made up of colors. Wherever light exists, color does, too. When there is no light, you "see" black. Black is the absence of light. It is not a color at all. You can see from the pictures that a tree that is green in light appears black at night, and that a shadow is black because a solid object blocks out the light.

Colors look different from each other because light moves much as waves do, and each color of light has a different *wavelength*. The wavelength is what makes red light different from waves of any other color. Light waves are very short. About 36,000 red waves cover only an inch (2.5 cm)! Violet has the shortest visible wavelength, and red has the longest. A single color is spread over a small band of wavelengths that cannot be separated by a prism.

You can easily see another type of color spectrum by looking at a white light through a silk scarf or any finely woven material, such as a handkerchief. The colors are brightest if you look at a small bright light at night or in a darkened room. The colorful pattern you see shows that light rays behave as waves, very much like ocean waves or sound waves. Sound waves go around corners, down halls, and through doors. Ocean waves flow around rocks and piers. Light waves curve around tiny objects, such as the fine scarf threads. Red light goes farther around solid objects than all the other colors

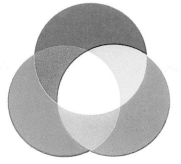

▲ The primary colors of pigments are cyan, yellow, and magenta.

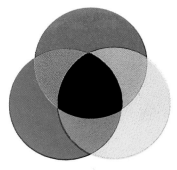

▲ The primary colors of light are blue, green, and red.

because its wave length is the longest. These different wavelengths of colors cause white light to break into spectacular *diffraction patterns* as the light passes tiny objects. You can see these lovely patterns in soap bubbles, raindrops, and oil slicks.

Kinds of Colors

Some people can see almost 100 colors in the spectrum. However, white light and any other color can be made by mixing different amounts of only three colors. These are called *primary* colors. Red, green, and blue form a group of primary colors of light. The colors in color television are made from different mixtures of these three colors. The color wheel for rays of light is shown in the picture.

Secondary colors are those made by mixing two primary colors together. These can be seen in the illustration—turquoise (blue-green), yellow, and magenta (purple-red). Yellow, for example, is made by mixing green and red primary colors of light. *Complementary* colors make white lights when two are mixed.

THE SPECTRUM

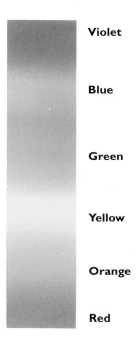

Violet

Blue

Green

Yellow

Orange

Red

▲ The color spectrum. A rainbow is a spectrum of light.

LEARN BY DOING

The colors that make up white light are called the *spectrum*. The main colors of the spectrum are red, orange, yellow, green, blue, and violet. You can make a spectrum of light colors by using water to form a *prism*. Put a small mirror in a glass of water so that it forms an angle. When sunlight hits the mirror, the short waves of violet are bent more than the other colors. Red is bent the least; the other colors fall in between.

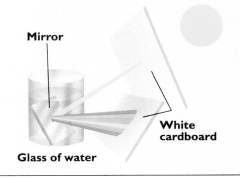

Mirror

White cardboard

Glass of water

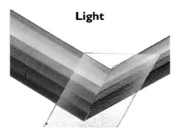

Light

White surface

Black surface

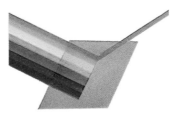

Red surface

▲ A white object reflects all the colors in light. A black object reflects no light but absorbs light. A red object reflects red, but absorbs the other colors.

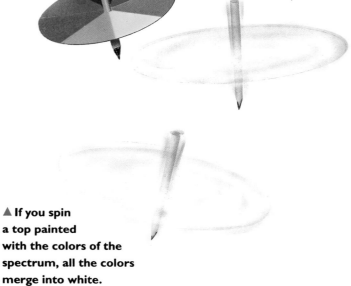

▲ If you spin a top painted with the colors of the spectrum, all the colors merge into white.

One of them must be primary and the other a secondary color. Blue and yellow are complementary colors. You can mix your own colored rays of light by shining flashlights through different colors of cellophane to make many beautiful colors of light.

The primary colors of pigments are *cyan* (blue-green), yellow, and *magenta* (purple-red). A *pigment* is the substance that gives an object its color. Grass, apples, hair, and paint, for example, are all pigmented. Transparent things, such as glass or water, have no pigment in them, so they are "colorless." The color of pigmented objects is named for the color that people see. Red paint soaks up or *absorbs* all of the colors in white light except red. Red paint bounces back, or *reflects* red, which is then the only visible color.

On the color wheel for pigments, or paint colors, complementary colors are opposite each other. If you could carefully mix the pure primary colors, you would see black. Any color of paint can be made from the primary colors. Colors are lightened to *tints* by adding white paint. Dark colors are made by adding black paint or paint of a complementary color.

▶▶▶▶ **FIND OUT MORE** ◀◀◀◀
Color Blindness; Light; Rainbow; Spectrum

 ## COLORADO

The name Colorado is a Spanish word meaning "red." Early Spanish explorers found reddish rock along a river that they discovered, so they named the river Colorado. The name was given, much later, to the state where the river begins.

The Land

It is easy to draw a map of Colorado because the state is a rectangle. The northern and southern boundaries are straight lines that run from west to east. The western and eastern boundaries are straight, too. They run from north to south.

Draw a vertical (north-south) line that divides your map of Colorado into two parts. Draw this line a little to the right (east) of the middle of the state. The dividing line is what we call "105 degrees west longitude," called the "105th meridian" for short. (*Meridians of longitude* are reference lines that run from the North Pole to the South Pole on globes and maps.)

The Rocky Mountains cover the state west of the meridian. This part of Colorado is high. The High Plains lie east of the dividing line. They *are* high, but still much lower than the mountains. The High Plains are a section of the Great Plains, an area that covers the United States from north to south and east to west in the center of the country. But they are hillier than most of the Great Plains.

The two parts of Colorado—western and eastern—slope in different directions. They do this because the ridge of the Rocky Mountains runs through the state. The Great Divide, also named the *Continental Divide*, is near the 105th meridian. Since rivers flow downhill, you can look at Colorado's rivers to learn the slope of the land.

The Colorado River flows through the mountainous part of the state. This river is on the western side of

STATE SYMBOLS

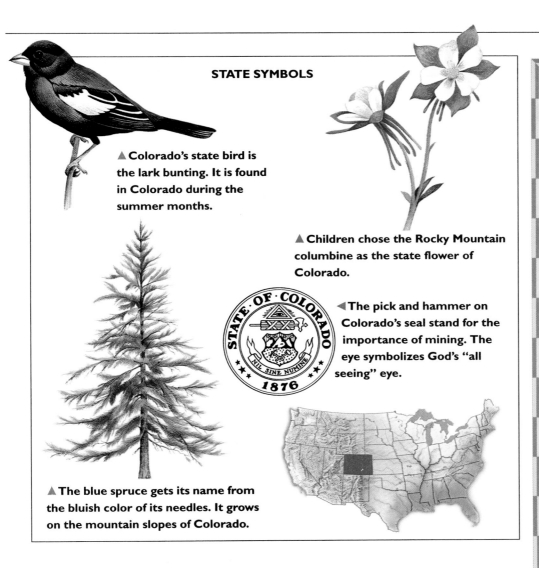

▲ Colorado's state bird is the lark bunting. It is found in Colorado during the summer months.

▲ Children chose the Rocky Mountain columbine as the state flower of Colorado.

◀ The pick and hammer on Colorado's seal stand for the importance of mining. The eye symbolizes God's "all seeing" eye.

▲ The blue spruce gets its name from the bluish color of its needles. It grows on the mountain slopes of Colorado.

COLORADO

Capital and largest city
Denver (467,610 people)

Area
104,247 square miles
(269,979 sq. km)
Rank: 8th

Population
3,294,394 people
Rank: 26th

Statehood
August 1, 1876
(38th state admitted)

Principle rivers
Colorado River
Arkansas River
South Platte River

Highest point
Mount Elbert,
14,433 feet (4,399 m)

Motto
Nil Sine Numine ("Nothing without Providence")

Song
"Where the Columbines Grow"

Famous people
Frederick Bonfils, M. Scott Carpenter, Douglas Fairbanks, Florence Rena Sabin, Lowell Thomas, Paul Whitman

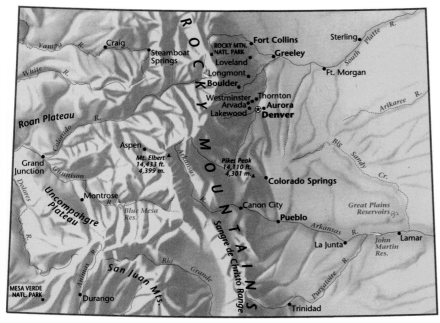

0   50   100 Miles
0   50   100   150 Kilometers

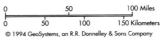

© 1994 GeoSystems, an R.R. Donnelley & Sons Company

▲ Cattle and sheep graze beneath the snow-covered peaks of Colorado's Rocky Mountains.

▲ The Colorado beetle, or potato bug, is native to the state. When early settlers planted potatoes in Colorado, the beetles began eating them.

One of Colorado's nicknames is the "Centennial State" because it joined the Union in 1876—just 100 years after the signing of the Declaration of Independence.

the Great Divide. The Colorado flows westward, so we know that the land slopes down to the west.

The Arkansas and South Platte rivers are east of the Great Divide. They flow eastward, showing that the land slopes that way. The High Plains at the base of the Rockies are about one mile (1.6 km) above the level of the sea. Near the border of Nebraska and Kansas on the eastern edge of the state, they are two-thirds of a mile (1.2 km) above sea level.

You can see both parts of Colorado from Denver, the state capital. Denver, often called the "mile-high city," is on the 105th meridian. The jagged wall of the Rockies is west of the city. Some nearby mountains are so high that snow covers them even in summer. East of Denver are the hills of the High Plains.

Climate

The state's climate is generally dry and sunny. However, because of differences in altitude, there can be extreme temperature differences within a short distance. For instance, in winter, the average temperature is about 29°F (-2°C) on the plains and about 11°F (-12°C) in the mountains. In summer, the average temperature is about 70°F (21°C) on the plains and about 55°F (13°C) in the moun-

tains. Colorado's highest temperature, 118°F (48°C) was recorded at Bennett on July 11, 1888. Its lowest occurred at Taylor Park Dam on Feb. 1, 1951: 60°F below zero (-51°C).

Differences in precipitation are great, too. The High Plains have the state's good farmland. But too little rain falls for most crops. Winter snow piles up in the mountains, where farming is impossible. But the snow melts in spring and summer, and water runs into the rivers. Those that flow eastward are used to irrigate the rich farming land of the High Plains.

History

France claimed what is now eastern Colorado in 1682. Spanish explorers visited this land and finally claimed the whole region for their king in 1706. The explorers found many Native Americans already living in the region. The Arapaho, Cheyenne, Comanche, Kiowa, and Pawnee tribes lived on the plains. The Utes lived in the valleys in the west.

France gained control of the whole region by a secret treaty with Spain. In 1803, the United States received the eastern half as part of the Louisiana Purchase. The western half became U.S. territory at the end of the Mexican War in 1848.

Gold was discovered ten years later in Cherry Creek (now in downtown Denver). Men from the East flocked to Colorado. Denver, Boulder, and Colorado City were among the first settlements.

The white men took land that the Native Americans had used for hunting. The Cheyenne and Arapaho of the plains fought to hold their hunting grounds. A group of soldiers attacked a Cheyenne village in 1864, in the battle now called the Sand Creek Massacre. Hundreds of Native American men, women, and children were killed.

The U.S. government criticized the soldiers' bloody attack. In the mountains, the Utes fought for their land, too. After many bitter fights, in which Native Americans and whites were killed, peace was finally made. Nearly all the Native Americans moved to reservations in other areas.

Colorado became the 38th state in 1876. Some of its people mined gold and silver in the mountains, and some raised sheep and cattle on the plains. But time brought changes. Other natural resources were discovered and mined. Irrigation brought farmers to the plains. People earned money and started some factories.

Coloradans at Work

Manufacturing is the top industry of Colorado now. Among the principal manufactured goods are machinery, food products, computer equipment, aerospace equipment, rubber, and steel. Denver, the capital, and Pueblo are the main industrial cities.

Pueblo has a huge steel industry. The city began in 1842 as a trading post owned by James P. Beckwourth, a black merchant. He named it *Pueblo* (Spanish for "town") because many of the people there were Mexicans.

Colorado has about 27,000 farms that range in size from large ranches to small vegetable farms. Cattle, sheep, and poultry are raised on the High Plains. The leading crops are wheat, corn, hay, and sugar beets.

Mining is a major industry in the state, which holds half the world's supply of *molybdenum* (a metal that hardens steel). Other minerals are petroleum, natural gas, coal, and uranium. Oil shale is Colorado's main undeveloped resource.

Tourism ranks among the state's top industries. Millions of visitors come to the state each year, attracted by Colorado's magnificent scenery, climate, and recreational facilities. Colorado has an average of 310 sunny days a year.

Rocky Mountain National Park covers 405 square miles (1,049 sq. km). The Great Divide runs through it. A fine road takes motorists more than two miles (3 km) above sea level. They can see ice fields glittering in summer sun. And they may catch sight of mountain lion, elk, black bear, and bighorn sheep. Mesa Verde (meaning "Green Table"), another famous national park, has houses built high into cliffs by Native Americans about 2,000 years ago. These houses were already very old when the first white men arrived.

Skiers visit such well-known resorts as Aspen, Vail, and Winter Park. Fishermen, big-game hunters, and mountain climbers are attracted to these and other places in summer.

▶ ▶ ▶ ▶ **FIND OUT MORE** ◀ ◀ ◀ ◀
Cliff Dwellers; Gold Rush; Indian Wars; Louisiana Purchase; Mexican War; Native Americans; Pike, Zebulon; Rio Grande; Westward Movement

Colorado is the highest state in the Union. Its average height is 6,800 feet (2,073 m) above sea level. The state has more than half of the highest peaks in the United States.

▲ **Giant sandstone formations reach into the sky in the Garden of the Gods near Colorado Springs.**

◀ **Colorado is a state of dramatic scenery. This is a summertime view of a mountain Lake, called Nymph lake, with Hallett Peak in the background.**

The English chemist John Dalton was the first to study color blindness scientifically. He was color blind himself, which he had discovered as a small boy. He was watching a parade one day and the people around him were talking about the soldiers' red uniforms. He had thought they were green!

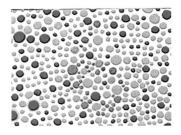

▲ A color blindness test card. If you have normal color vision you should be able to see the number 6.

▲ The Columbia River is one of the longest and most important rivers in North America.

COLOR BLINDNESS

Some people do not distinguish colors as clearly as other people. These individuals are said to be *color blind*. You must first understand how you see colors to understand what is meant by color blindness.

White light, or sunlight, is really a combination of different colors—red, orange, yellow, green, blue, and violet. Each of these colors can be produced by mixing three primary colors of light—red, green, and blue—in the right amounts. At the back of the eye is a type of screen called the *retina*. Some cells of the retina are sensitive to red, some to green, and some to blue light. When white light falls on the retina, it stimulates all three cell types more or less equally. The result is that you see white light. You see other colors when the retina cells are stimulated in unequal amounts. For example, you see a yellow color when the red and green cells are equally stimulated and the blue cells stimulated only slightly.

Color blindness occurs when the sensitivity of the retina to any one of these colors is damaged. For example, when the cells sensitive to red are effected, a person cannot see red in quite the same way as a person whose sensitivity to red is normal. People who have the commonest types of color blindness generally see red and green as different degrees of yellow, but they see other colors normally. Some people cannot see any color at all. Their world appears black, white, and gray. Color blindness affects men more than women. A color-blind person may be unaware of his condition unless his color vision is tested. It is important to detect color blindness since a person who confuses red and green, for example, may have trouble recognizing traffic signals.

▶▶▶ **FIND OUT MORE** ◀◀◀
Color; Eye; Light; Sight

COLUMBIA RIVER

The Columbia River begins high in the ice and snow of the Canadian Rocky Mountains in British Columbia. It streams through mountain passes as it flows southward across the U.S. border into Washington state. Then it curves westward to empty into the Pacific Ocean at Astoria, Oregon. The Columbia River forms most of the boundary between the states of Washington and Oregon.

Robert Gray, an American sea captain, discovered the mouth of the river in 1792, while he was cruising along the Oregon coast in his ship, the *Columbia*. He named the river after the ship. The American explorers Meriwether Lewis and William Clark paddled their canoes through the rapids of the Columbia River to reach the Pacific in 1805. Within six years, another explorer, David Thompson, had traveled the entire 1,214 miles (1,954 km) of the Columbia, from source to mouth.

More than 25 dams have been built on the Columbia and its many tributaries. Among the largest are the Grand Coulee, Bonneville, John Day, McNary, and the Dalles. These dams harness the river's flow to make electricity. It is the largest source of electricity in the northwestern United States. They also make the water flow into irrigation canals and form lakes where people can sail boats and swim.

Because of the dams, oceangoing ships can travel up the river only as far as Portland, Oregon. Small boats go around the dams by using canals, part of a 328-mile (528-km) slackwater navigation channel up the river. The Columbia River salmon get around the dams by jumping up "fish ladders." A fish ladder provides a water stairway for fish that go upstream to lay their eggs.

▶▶▶ **FIND OUT MORE** ◀◀◀
British Columbia; Dam; Oregon; River; Washington

COLUMBUS, CHRISTOPHER (1451–1506)

Christopher Columbus was a courageous seafarer who followed his dream of exploring unknown places. He opened the New World—North and South America—to all of Europe.

Columbus was born in Genoa, Italy, the son of a weaver. His name in Italian was Cristoforo Colombo. He was also called Cristóbal Colón when he sailed under the flag of Spain. Columbus made many voyages to the Gold Coast of Africa in his youth. He believed that Asia could be reached by heading west. He thought that Japan was only about 3,000 miles (5,600 km) west of Europe. (In fact, it is over 11,000 miles [20,400 km]). Europeans wanted an easier way to get Asia's wealth of gold, silk, and spices than by slow caravans crossing great mountains and deserts. Mapmakers and seamen thought that the voyage would be impossible.

Columbus tried to persuade King John I of Portugal to give him money for ships, but John refused. So Columbus went to Spain. After six years, Queen Isabella agreed to provide money for the expedition, and three ships sailed from Spain on August 3, 1492. They were the *Niña*, the *Pinta*, and the *Santa Maria*, which Columbus commanded. The voyage was difficult. The men grew discouraged and almost mutinied as they sailed farther and farther from home. Land was finally sighted on October 12. Columbus named the land San Salvador, claiming it for Spain. San Salvador was actually an island in the Bahamas, but Columbus always

▼ Christopher Columbus landed on an island in the Bahamas, which he named San Salvador. He met with no resistance from the Arawaks who lived there and Columbus ordered his men to treat these people well.

believed he had found the "Indies," and as a result he called the people there "Indians." Upon his return to Spain, he was greeted with joy and given many honors.

Columbus made three more voyages, in 1493, 1498, and 1502. He established settlements and discovered new islands each time. Troubles in the colonies led to Columbus's arrest in 1500. He was soon pardoned, but his enemies were able to reduce the amount of money he was given for his fourth and last voyage. Columbus returned to Spain tired and ill from this voyage in 1504. He spent the last few months of his life trying to collect the rewards that were due to him, but he died in poverty. Years later Columbus's grandson had his body moved to Santo Domingo, in the Dominican Republic, where it now lies in the cathedral of Santa Maria.

▶▶▶▶ **FIND OUT MORE** ◀◀◀◀
America; Exploration; Vikings

▼ Columbus's banner bore a cross and symbols of the king and queen of Spain.

◀ An early drawing of a pineapple—one of the first fruits Columbus discovered in the West Indies.

On Christmas Eve, 1492, a cabin boy was at the helm of the *Santa Maria* when the ship was wrecked. Columbus had to sail home to Spain in the *Niña*, beating the *Pinta*, the other ship of his fleet, by only a few hours.

COMANCHES

The Comanches were nomads of the Great Plains. They hunted *bison* (buffalo) as they wandered through land that is now Nebraska, Kansas, Oklahoma, Colorado, and Texas.

The Comanches were the best horsemen of all the Native Americans. They rode bareback (without a saddle). Each warrior braided a loop of horse hair into his horse's mane. If he was shot at, the warrior could slip his body into the loop and ride down against his horse's side, with only one leg hooked over the top of his horse. Soldiers and pioneers claimed that a Comanche warrior could shoot as well from this horizontal position as he could sitting up on his horse.

▲ Quanah Parker, famous Comanche chief. His first name means "sweet smelling one." He got his last name from his white mother.

▲ A Comanche warrior ropes a wild stallion in a painting by the famous artist, George Catling.

Horses were so important to the Comanche tribe that they became a kind of money. A wealthy man would own several hundred horses. He could exchange a good horse for weapons and food. The Comanches roamed far and wide, always on the lookout for wild horses to catch and tame. Their buffalo-hide tepees were easily moved, so they could quickly pack up to follow the buffalo herd on which they depended for food and clothing.

As the white man moved west, he killed thousands and thousands of bison. The Comanches fought to save their land and way of life. But soon they could not find enough food by hunting. They signed a peace treaty with the United States government in 1867 and moved to a reservation in what is now the state of Oklahoma. Today, many of the approximately 7,500 Comanches that live in the United States work as businessmen, ranchers, and farmers.

▶▶▶▶ **FIND OUT MORE** ◀◀◀◀
Bison; Indian Wars; Native Americans

COMB JELLY

Comb jellies are among the oddest animals in the ocean. They look like transparent jellyfish and are usually round or oval. One kind of comb jelly is the *sea walnut*. Another is the *sea gooseberry*, or cat's eye, which is often washed onto beaches. You might find some about the size of a marble. Try placing a few cat's eyes in a pail of sea water. If they are not dead, they will swim around.

Varieties of comb jellies live in oceans over most of the world, but most kinds inhabit warm waters. They are greedy eaters. They snare prey, such as fish and fish eggs, with sticky, hairy tentacles.

If you see them swim, you will notice tiny hairlike structures, called *cilia*, beat the water rapidly, moving the animals forward like tiny paddleboats. Eight sets of the cilia are arranged like teeth on a comb. The beating of the cilia refracts light in the water, making rainbow colors as the animal swims. Comb jellies shine at night, making the water around them green and luminous.

Comb jellies form a group, or *phylum*, called the *Ctenophora*. Some of the 80 varieties are quite beautiful. One kind, *Venus's girdle*, is shaped like a ribbon and may grow to be 4 feet (1.2 m) in length.

▶▶▶▶ **FIND OUT MORE** ◀◀◀◀
Animal Kingdom

COMBUSTION

SEE FIRE

COMETS

Comets are the strange nomads of the solar system that travel around the sun in very *elongated*, or stretched out, paths. A comet first appears as a faint, moving spot far out in space. As it nears the sun, it becomes brighter and may grow a tail. After it passes the sun, it begins to dim, and any tail formed soon disappears.

Some comets are seen every few years because their orbits are small, perhaps taking them only as far out as the planet Jupiter. These are too faint to be seen easily with the naked eye. The very bright comets move in much larger orbits and may take thousands of years to go around once. These often develop fine tails, but they move so quickly when near the sun that they may only be seen with the naked eye for a few weeks.

The small solid *nucleus,* or center, of a comet is made mostly of water ice and frozen ammonia, methane, and carbon dioxide, all mixed with dust particles. In 1986 the *Giotto* space probe photographed the nucleus of Halley's Comet as a "peanut" about 9 miles (15 km) long. The tail forms when the ice is turned to vapor by the sun's heat, and dust particles are also released. A comet's tail may be millions of miles long and always points away from the sun because the sun's heat pushes the tail away from it.

People have been watching comets for many centuries. In 1705, the Eng-

lish astronomer Edmund Halley noted that the description of three comets—which had been seen in 1531, 1607, and 1682—were very much alike. Halley thought that it might really be just one comet, appearing again and again. If it were, he figured, it would appear again in about 75 or 76 years, or in 1758. It did, and the comet was named after him. Halley's Comet was spectacular in 1835 and 1910, but in 1986 it seemed faint, because the Earth was in the wrong part of its orbit for the best view.

▶▶▶▶ **FIND OUT MORE** ◀◀◀◀
Orbit; Solar System; Space

▲ The nucleus of Halley's Comet is a peanut-shaped mixture of rock, dust, and ice.

The European *Giotto* and two former Soviet *Vega* space probes showed details of the "dirty snowball" nucleus of Halley's Comet. They found that the dust coming off the nucleus contains complex carbon compounds. The nucleus of the comet was found to be about 9 miles (15 km) long, 5 miles (7.5 km) wide, and 5 miles (7.5 km) thick. Its surface is very black.

◀ The *Giotto* space probe.

COMICS

Every day millions of children and adults all over the world read their favorite comics, or "funnies," in their daily newspapers.

Most comics consist of a set of black and white or color drawings that tell a funny, exciting, or dramatic story. In a comic, what the character says or thinks is drawn in a "balloon" above him or her.

Artists draw comics for people of all ages and interests. Some comics are truly "funnies" that present characters who do and say funny things. One example is the comic strip *Blondie,* by Dean Young and Stan Drake, which shows the amusing adventures of Blondie and her bumbling husband, Dagwood Bumstead. *Garfield* by Jim Davis presents the antics of a funny cat. Another kind

WHERE TO DISCOVER MORE

Cummings, Richard. *Make Your Own Comics for Fun & Profit.* New York: McKay, 1985.

▲ The amusing adventures of Charlie Brown are told in *Peanuts,* one of the most popular of all comic strips. It was created in 1950 by a cartoonist from Minnesota, Charles Schulz.

Norman Rockwell was probably the best-known American illustrator. He gained great popularity as a cover illustrator for *The Saturday Evening Post* and other magazines. Rockwell also worked for many advertisers during his long life—he died in 1978 at the age of 84.

▼ This 1923 poster advertising Coca-Cola is a striking example of commercial art.

is the adventure comic strip, which leaves its readers "hanging" in suspense so that they will be sure to buy the next day's paper to find out what happens. Hal Foster's *Prince Valiant,* by John Cullen Murphy, is an adventure strip about the exciting life of a young nobleman in the days of King Arthur. The fantastic, impossible adventures of a bigger-than-life hero, *Superman*, by Jerry Siegel, began as a comic strip but gained popularity in comic books and movies.

Comic strips have been read and enjoyed for more than 75 years. *Hogan's Alley,* by Richard F. Outcault, was published in 1896. *Hogan's Alley* was not actually a true comic strip, but really a fun-page drawing.

Comic strips are printed in newspapers all over the world, but the "funnies" are most popular in the United States. A famous artist once said that the most original American art form is comics. Comics appear in almost every American newspaper. Artists sell their comics to a *syndicate,* a company that sells the comics to all newspapers that want to print them. Other comics are printed in books called comic books.

▶▶▶▶ **FIND OUT MORE** ◀◀◀◀
Cartooning; Commercial Art; Design; Drawing; Graphic Arts; Newspaper

COMMERCIAL ART

Have you ever painted a poster advertising a school fair? If you have, you have made some commercial art. The word *commercial* comes from commerce, which means business. Commercial art, then, is that art which has to do with business.

The Romans had commercial art over two thousand years ago. They put signs over shops so that people could tell what was sold inside. A huge shoe would hang outside a shoemaker's shop, for example.

Commercial artists must be able to design, draw, and paint well. They often receive training at an art school or college. They learn how to lay out magazines and books—that is, where to put the pictures and columns of type, how to arrange everything on a page. They learn how to design jackets for books and how to illustrate them. Some commercial artists learn mechanical drawing or *drafting* (drawing of architectural or engineering diagrams), map and chart drawing, *graphic arts* (print making, engraving, etching), and cartooning.

Commercial artists, working with a special writer called a *copywriter,* prepare advertisements for magazines and newspapers, and commercials for television. They also illustrate books. Fashion designers design clothing, and industrial designers, working with engineers, design the shapes of appliances and many other products.

▶▶▶▶ **FIND OUT MORE** ◀◀◀◀
Advertising; Cartooning; Design; Fashion; Graphic Arts; Mechanical Drawing

COMMONWEALTH OF INDEPENDENT STATES

The Commonwealth of Independent States (CIS) is an association of 11 republics that had been part of the Soviet Union. It was established on December 21, 1991. The Soviet Union ceased to exist four days later. CIS members are independent, but have agreed to cooperate on many economic and military matters.

The capital of the CIS is Minsk, in Belarus. CIS members are Armenia, Azerbaijan, Belarus, Kazakhstan, Kyrgyzstan, Moldova, Russia, Tajikistan, Turkmenistan, Ukraine, and Uzbekistan. The other four former Soviet republics (Estonia, Georgia, Latvia, and Lithuania) chose not to join the CIS.

▶▶▶▶ **FIND OUT MORE** ◀◀◀◀
See the articles on individual countries.

COMMONWEALTH OF NATIONS

If you live in Canada, you are a member of an independent country that governs itself much like the United States. But it is also part of the Commonwealth of Nations. This is a group of countries that were once all part of the British Empire. Britain does not govern them any more, but they continue to use systems of law based on those of Britain, and have a common interest in each other. Member nations of the Commonwealth talk over problems and have agreements for trade and defense.

Between the 1600s and the early 1900s, Great Britain acquired many overseas territories. These lands paid allegiance to the British *monarch* (king or queen). At its peak, the British Empire ruled so many colonies all around the globe that a common saying was, "The sun never sets on the British Empire." In the late 1800s, it included nearly 16 million square miles (41 million sq. km) and more than 500 million people.

After the 13 American colonies revolted in 1776, the British Empire lost much of its land. However, new *territories* in the Pacific Ocean were later added to the empire, as were lands in Africa.

In the later decades of the 1800s, Britain gave some independence to its colonies, notably to Canada, Australia, and New Zealand. Increasingly, territories started demanding more political and economic freedom. In 1931, the full independence of Canada, Australia, New Zealand and South Africa was recognized by law. After World War II, Britain granted independence to India, a country it had ruled for almost 200 years, and many of its other colonies in Asia, Africa, and the Americas.

By the 1970s, Britain had given up most of its overseas territories. Nearly all of these newly independent nations joined the Commonwealth. (The Republic of Ireland and South Africa withdrew from it; Pakistan withdrew in 1972 but rejoined in 1989.) In 1990, the Commonwealth had 50 independent members and more than 20 other members.

Britain's Queen Elizabeth II is head of state of the United Kingdom (Britain) and 16 other countries. She is also head of the Commonwealth, but she does not have any real power. She is a symbol, or representative, of the Commonwealth. Each of the member countries in the Commonwealth chooses its own government and makes its own decisions on things like peace and war.

▶▶▶▶ **FIND OUT MORE** ◀◀◀◀
Colony; English History

INDEPENDENT MEMBERS OF THE COMMONWEALTH OF NATIONS

Antigua and Barbuda, Australia, Bahamas, Bangladesh, Barbados, Belize, Botswana, Brunei, Canada, Cyprus, Dominica, The Gambia, Ghana, Grenada, Guyana, India, Jamaica, Kenya, Kiribati, Lesotho, Malawi, Malaysia, Malta, Maldives, Mauritius, Namibia, Nauru, New Zealand, Nigeria, Pakistan, Papua New Guinea, St. Kitts-Nevis, St. Lucia, St. Vincent and the Grenadines, Seychelles, Sierra Leone, Singapore, Solomon Islands, Sri Lanka, Swaziland, Tanzania, Tonga, Trinidad and Tobago, Tuvalu, Uganda, United Kingdom, Vanuatu, Western Samoa, Zambia, Zimbabwe

The dependencies belonging to Australia, India, New Zealand, and the United Kingdom are also part of the Commonwealth.

◀ The emblems of two Commonwealth members: Australia (top) and New Zealand (bottom).

▲ **An ancient Egyptian papyrus with hieroglyphics.**

▲ **Johannes Gutenberg checking a printed sheet.**

▼ **An early newspaper,** *The Antwerp Gazette.*

COMMUNICATION

Communication is an exchange of information, feelings, attitudes, or ideas. Many animals communicate with one another, but humans have the most complicated system of communication. Speech, writing, books, magazines, mail, telephone, radio, computers, and television all work together to set human beings apart from every other living thing. Without communication there would be no recorded history, no development of civilization, no organization of society, and no learning. Each new generation would have to discover and invent everything again.

Every time you talk to your family or to a friend, you are communicating by *speech,* the earliest and still the most important kind of human communication. We will never know how or when speech began, we can only guess. The earliest people probably communicated much like other animals, with grunts. Hundreds of thousands of years ago, people somehow learned to use sounds, each of which meant something special to other people. They slowly learned to put the sounds together to form language.

But people still could not communicate over distances, and they had no way of recording words. People began to use runners to solve the first problem but this was very slow. So people kept trying to find faster ways to carry messages.

Written Communication

To solve the second problem, people first invented ways of making pictures, from which picture writing developed. The first people to do this were the Sumerians, in about 3500 B.C. Soon after that, the ancient Egyptians developed another important picture writing, called *hieroglyphics.* The first alphabet was developed by the Semites of Syria, especially the Phoenicians, in about 1300 B.C. The symbols of the alphabet stood for sounds rather than words.

People were soon busy writing, first on clay tablets, then on rolled-up sheets or scrolls of *papyrus* made from reeds (plant fiber) and later on *parchment* made from animal skin. People began to change from scrolls to books around A.D. 200. Books were much easier to read and store. But like scrolls, each book had to be lettered by hand, and they were expensive.

Printing is one of the greatest inventions. The oldest known printed work is a scroll printed with carved wooden blocks in Korea in about A.D. 700. Europeans did not use printing until the fifteenth century. Johannes Gutenberg, a German, introduced printing to Europe. He developed a usable system of movable type around 1440. With Gutenberg's system, each letter was a separate piece. A book page could be made up of type *set* in a frame, and many copies could be made. Books could be produced more quickly and cheaply, so that many more people could read and learn from the communication of others.

Printing also brought about new forms of communication, especially newspapers and magazines. Newspapers as we know them today began in the seventeenth century, magazines in the eighteenth century.

Modern Devices

Developments in transport such as the railway, improved roads, canals, and steam-powered ships, also speeded up communication. These inventions helped transform the time it took to deliver mail.

Near the mid 1800s, the invention of cameras and plates (later film) allowed people to make an exact visual record of what they saw. At the end of the century, inventors devised ways to show movement on film by making motion pictures.

The discovery of electricity made

▼ **Marconi sent the first Morse code signals across the Atlantic in 1901.**

communication over huge distances possible. The telegraph was the first communication device to use electricity. It sent signals over wires. Samuel F. B. Morse sent the first message by telegraph in 1844. Wires were later used to send the human voice over a long distance. Alexander Graham Bell patented this new device, the telephone, in 1876. Guglielmo Marconi first demonstrated the "wireless," or radio, in 1895.

People have also learned how to make a permanent record of sound, just as they learned to make written and visual records. Thomas Edison invented the phonograph in 1877. Later, sound recordings were combined with moving pictures.

In the 1900s, people have invented other devices to help them communicate. Television uses electricity to transmit sound and pictures. Communications satellites in space are used to relay television and other kinds of communications from one place to anywhere else in the world.

Computers that process information with awesome speed have given communication another huge push forward. With a computer, people can store, process, and print information faster than ever before and in enormous quantities. Some computers can print a million words in as little as a minute and store the words on a single disc only a few inches across.

Uses of Communication

People have become fascinated by communication, and scientists have begun to study it. One important fact that scientists have discovered is that many animals communicate, too. Bees and other insects "tell" one another where flowers are blooming by performing movements like a dance when they return to the hive. Birds sing and call to one another with various meanings. And dolphins appear to communicate by using a very complicated language.

Scientists divide human communication into *personal* and *mass* communication. A message is carried from *sender* to *receiver* by a *channel* or *medium*. Personal communication takes place whenever one person exchanges ideas with another. In mass communication, one person (or a group of people) sends a message to many people whom the sender never

▲ **Many organizations now use video for training new recruits. By recording lectures and demonstrations on tape, they can be replayed many times over to different groups.**

▲ The Intelsat communications satellite can carry up to 33,000 simultaneous telephone conversations.

sees. Its channels, called *mass media,* include newspapers, books, radio, television, films, and recordings.

Every successful communication has five parts. These five parts can best be expressed in the following question, Who says what to whom through what channel or medium, and what is the result? If you do not understand what someone says, communication fails.

People have more and better ways to communicate now than ever before. But many problems—both personal and worldwide—are caused because people still do not always understand one another. Scientists continue to learn more about the process of communication.

▶▶▶▶ FIND OUT MORE ◀◀◀◀
Animal Communication see Animal Voices; Dolphins and Porpoises
History see Ancient Civilizations; Bell, Alexander Graham; Gutenberg, Johannes; Marconi, Guglielmo; Morse, Samuel F. B.; Radio Broadcasting; Sumer; Television Broadcasting
Language see Alphabet; Hieroglyphics; Languages; Written Language
Modern Devices see Computer; Radio; Facsimile (FAX); Photocopier; Telecommunications; Telegraph; Telephone; Television
Printing see Book; Magazine; Newspaper; Printing; Publishing; Typesetting

▼ A communications satellite can pass telephone messages, television programs and computer data between relay stations on different continents.

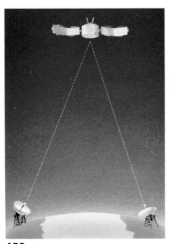

⚙ COMMUNICATIONS SATELLITE

Television covers sports and news around the world. Until 1964, reporters in distant countries had to race to the nearest airport with their news film. An airplane carried the film to the United States. This could take from half a day to several days,

and the film report was old news by the time it appeared on television. Telephone calls across the ocean were hard to make because the calls went by cables that lay on the ocean floor. But there weren't always enough cables, so people often waited hours. Satellites used for communication have changed that. The first one was put into orbit around Earth in 1964.

Today, television stations show videotapes of news events in other countries on the same day the event happens. Events can even be broadcast "live," no matter where in the world they happen. And telephone calls to almost any country in the world take just a minute or two.

Communications satellites *orbit,* or circle, the Earth about 22,300 miles (35,900 km) above the equator. A satellite stays above one place on the Earth's surface because the satellite takes the same time to orbit the Earth as the Earth takes to turn once.

A communications satellite is a relay station, or switchboard, in space. Television reaches the United States from Europe through the switchboard. First, the signal goes by cable to a ground station in Europe. The station antenna *transmits* (sends) the signal over radio waves in a straight line to a satellite above the Atlantic Ocean. The satellite automatically sends the signal back down to the antenna at a station in the United States. Finally, the signal goes by cable to the television network. The whole trip takes one-fourth of a second. Japan is farther from the U.S. than Europe, so two satellites are needed to get a signal from the U.S. to Japan.

Satellites relay telephone calls the same way. One satellite can carry many more calls than one telephone cable. It is now easier and cheaper to talk to people around the world.

▶▶▶▶ FIND OUT MORE ◀◀◀◀
Orbit; Satellite; Space Research; Telephone

COMMUNISM

The idea of Communism is very ancient. But Communism, as it is known today, first became popular in Europe in the 1800s. Put very simply, communism is a system of government in which everything is owned indirectly by all the people, and controlled by the state, or central government.

Communism grew out of the misery and poverty that existed in Europe starting in the mid-1800s, after the Industrial Revolution. During this time, factories replaced many small businesses. Factory bosses often treated their workers harshly. Employees had to work long hours in dangerous conditions for small wages.

Two German scholars, Karl Marx and Friedrich Engels, wrote a book called the *Communist Manifesto* in 1848. Marx and Engels believed all people should work for the common good. They made popular the Communist motto, "from each according to his ability, to each according to his need." They wrote of a "classless society" in which no single group of people would be more powerful than any other.

Marx hoped people would one day be able to live together without a central government. But many Communist governments became extremely powerful, owning most of their nation's property and industry. The freedom of the individual was thought to be less important than the good of the country. As a result, people were not free to believe or behave as they wished.

The Communists, unlike the Socialists who shared similar ideas, believed in revolution and violence to accomplish their goals. The first major Communist revolution took place in Russia in 1917. It was led by Vladimir (sometimes called Nikolai) Lenin.

Communist Russia eventually swallowed up the countries around it, forming the powerful Soviet

▲ Giant posters of Chinese Communist Party leaders formed the backdrop to a Party meeting in 1949.

Union. Countries in Eastern Europe and in many other parts of the world also became Communist nations. After a civil war, China became a Communist country in 1949.

Mikhail Gorbachev became leader of the Soviet Union in 1985. He set about reforming the Soviet Union and introduced more openness. These reforms led to the Communists losing control of the Soviet Union. It ceased to exist in 1991. In eastern Europe, too, people overthrew their communist rulers and established democratic governments.

▶▶▶▶ **FIND OUT MORE** ◀◀◀◀
China; Economics; Industrial Revolution; Lenin, Nikolai; Marx, Karl; Russia; Socialism; Soviet Union

▼ Some important Communist leaders. They are, clockwise from top left, Leon Trotsky, Vladimir Lenin, Mao Zedong, Josef Stalin, and Friedrich Engels. Trotsky and Engels were important figures in the Russian Revolution; Stalin was leader of the Soviet Union from 1924 to 1953; and Mao Zedong was Chairman of the People's Republic of China from 1949 to 1976.

COMMUNITY

Animals or people who live together as a group form a community. In the animal world, communities include packs of wolves, herds of elephants, and prides of lions. Social insects, such as bees in their hives and ants in their colonies, also form communities.

Most people belong to several communities. The *family* community usually has parents and children. The

▼ Community buying and selling flourishes unchanged in a market in Benares, India, where traders still sell grain as they have for centuries.

▼ Tokyo—a modern city—resembles many other modern cities. Cities are large, dense communities; within them are a collection of smaller communities.

neighborhood community is the area where the family lives. People also belong to the *state* community, the *national* community, and the *world*, or international community. Each of these communities is part of the next larger community.

The people of a community have similar ways and customs. For example, people in a neighborhood live in similar houses and apartments, and most people speak the same language. A community is usually in a definite space—a house at a certain address, a state with a name and boundaries, a nation covering a particular area of the globe, a world at a certain spot in the universe.

Each community is run by rules or laws. A family decides when children have to go to bed, or what time to have dinner. A state has laws such as who must go to school and for how many years. And each community

has certain activities or problems that unite it. For example, all the people in a neighborhood on the shore of an ocean may earn their living by fishing. People in a jungle village might get together to protect themselves from wild animals.

The earliest communities of people started thousands of years ago. Ancient peoples were hunters who were always searching for food. People hunted animals, fished, and gathered wild plants and fruit. If they could not collect enough food, they starved. Then, perhaps 12,000 years ago, people discovered they could raise crops. Somebody, probably in the region that is now Syria and Iraq, noticed that plants grew where seeds had fallen. People began settling down in one spot, in communities. Some people planted seeds and farmed, while others hunted.

One of the earliest permanent communities was a town later called Jericho, located in what is now Israel. The people who settled there built mud houses and put up a wall around their town. They dug irrigation ditches to water their crops of wheat, barley, and flax.

Now that they had finally settled down in one spot, people found that they could raise animals and kill them for food. People who did not grow food, such as shopkeepers, artists, and priests, were able to trade their services with the farmers for food. Farming communities gradually sprang up all along the Tigris and Euphrates rivers (now in Syria and Iraq), and along the Nile River in Egypt. The fertile land along the river meant that the farmers had no reason to move anymore. Generation after generation of people stayed in the same place.

Finally, too many people were trying to live off the narrow strips of good land along the banks of the rivers. Some had to move back from the best farming areas. People tried to improve the soil by burning vegetation and using the ashes as fertilizer.

But this process took a lot of time, and many farmers gave up. They left their villages and went elsewhere, burning forests and planting seeds between the burned stumps. They finally blazed their way through most of the forests of central Europe.

Some of the early farm communities, however, proved to be quite permanent. These farmers grew fruits, such as olives, dates, figs, and grapes. But the wheat farmers were constantly moving. These wheat farmers have been called *Danubians* because they followed the route of the Danube River. They made their way into Russia, Denmark, Sweden, and England. Others settled along the Swiss lakes and built houses on the water on piles of wood. Still other Danubians formed communities along the banks of the River Rhine.

People today have many more communities than they had thousands of years ago. Towns, cities, states, and nations are spread out in an ever-growing world community. But the first two communities—the family and the neighborhood—are still very much with us. And they are still the same, in many ways, as they were thousands of years ago.

▶▶▶▶ **FIND OUT MORE** ◀◀◀◀
Community Activities see Clubs and Societies; Fire Fighting; Hospital; Museum; Police; Postal Service; Public Health; Public Utility; School; Social Work
General Community Life see Citizenship; Communication; Crime; Juvenile Delinquency; Law; Safety; Shelter; Traffic Planning; Transportation
History see Ancient Civilizations; Culture; Customs; Feudalism; Native Americans; Pioneer Life
Kinds of Communities see City; Colony; County; International Relations; Local Government; Nation; Suburb

COMOROS

Comoros is a group of islands forming a volcanic *archipelago* (cluster of islands) in the Indian Ocean between north Madagascar and East Africa. Njazidja (which was called Grand Comoro until 1977) is the largest island. It has an active volcano, Mont Kartala, which erupted in 1977, making 20,000 people homeless.

The islands have a tropical climate. Most people are poor and earn their living from farming. Most of the farms are small and yields are generally low, because the soils are infertile. The export crops, including vanilla, copra, and cloves, are grown on large plantations. The official languages are Arabic and French, but most people speak Comoran, a mixture of the East African language Swahili and Arabic.

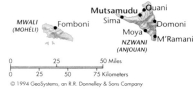

Arabs ruled the islands until the French gained control of them in 1886. In 1975, France granted independence to the largely Muslim islands of Njazidja and Nzwani (formerly called Anjouan), and Mwali (formerly Mohéli). These islands now form the Federal Islamic Republic of the Comoros. The fourth major island, Mayotte, is populated mainly by Christians. The people chose to remain under French control.

▶▶▶▶ **FIND OUT MORE** ◀◀◀◀
Africa; Indian Ocean

COMOROS

Capital city
Moroni (21,000 people)

Area
838 square miles
(2,171 sq. km)

Population
459,000 people

Government
Federal Islamic Republic

Natural resources
Negligible

Export products
Vanilla, copra, cloves, essential oils for use in perfume

Unit of money
Comorian franc

Official languages
Arabic, French

More than half the total value of exports from Comoros comes from vanilla, the flavoring that is used in ice cream, chocolate, pastry, and candy. The vanilla plant is a climbing orchid that makes its seeds in pods. The pods are picked before they are ripe. Then they are dried, chopped up, and soaked in alcohol and water to make vanilla essence. The word *vanilla* is Spanish for "little pod."

▼ In a compact disc player, the laser beam picks up signals from the tiny pits on the surface of the disc. The beam is reflected off the surface of the disc and the signals are changed back into the original, recorded sound.

☼ COMPACT DISC

A compact disc, often called a CD, is about 5 inches (12 cm) across but can play over an hour of music.

The disc contains a digital recording of music. This means that the sound is recorded in the form of code

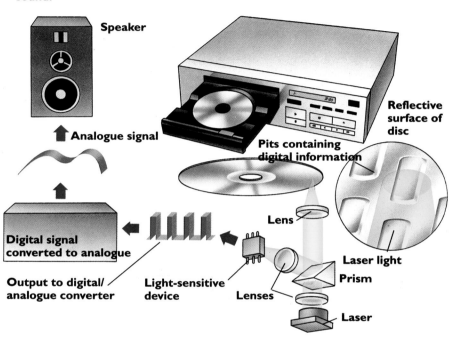

Speaker

Analogue signal

Digital signal converted to analogue

Output to digital/ analogue converter

Light-sensitive device

Lenses

Lens

Reflective surface of disc

Pits containing digital information

Laser light

Prism

Laser

▶ An early European compass.

▼ The Earth acts like a giant magnet, with its poles near, but not at, the North and South Poles.

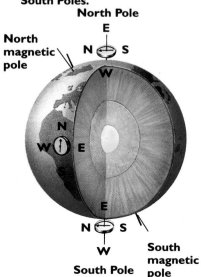

North Pole
E
North magnetic pole
N S
W
W
N
W E
E
N S
W
South Pole
South magnetic pole

signals. The codes consist of millions of patterns of tiny pits on the surface of the disc. In a compact disc player, a laser beam of light moves across the disc as it spins and is reflected by the tiny surface pits. The reflected beam carries the signals, which are then changed into the music. Because there is no abrasive contact between the disc and the beam, there is no wear on the disc. The quality is good because digital recordings are less likely to be distorted.

A CD-ROM (compact disc-read only memory) is a compact disk for a computer. The disc holds words, video, music, and photos. A CD-I (compact disc-interactive) is used with a television to play games and music.

▶▶▶▶ **FIND OUT MORE** ◀◀◀◀
Computer; Recording

☼ COMPASS

Voyages of exploration and treks through unmapped wilderness would have been much more difficult without the simple device called the compass. A compass is a direction finder. Most compasses consist of a short, flat, thin, arrow-shaped piece of metal that is balanced on the point of a short rod. The rod sticks up from a circular card on which are printed the directions—north (N), south (S), east (E), and west (W). The piece of metal is a *magnet*. It can swing around on the rod, so the arrowhead points northward and the tail of the arrow points southward. This happens because the Earth itself is a huge magnet, and one magnet always acts with force upon another.

Compasses are used in navigation. The Chinese were among the first to use the compass, and European sailors were using them by the 1100s. These sailors knew about a kind of iron ore called *lodestone,* which is a natural

magnet. The first compasses they used were needle-shaped pieces of lodestone hanging by a thread.

Sailors also learned that they could make a magnet from an iron needle stroked on lodestone. They thrust the needle through a piece of reed or cork and floated it in water. One end of the needle always turned to the north.

The North Magnetic Pole
Although the Earth's magnetism makes one end of a compass needle

▲ **A traditional mariner's compass used aboard a ship or boat.**

point northward, the needle does not point straight to the North Pole, but to the north magnetic pole. This is a point located in the Canadian Northwest Territories, several hundred miles south of the actual North Pole. But the error of the compass can be corrected because navigators have measured the variations for almost all places on the Earth.

A *gyrocompass* is one that can be made to point always true north, or any other direction wanted. It consists of a *gyroscope* mounted so that it can swing freely. The gyroscope's wheel is started spinning and is pointed straight north. No matter in what direction a ship, airplane, or rocket turns, the gyrocompass mounted on it continues to point to the direction in which it was set.

▶▶▶▶ **FIND OUT MORE** ◀◀◀◀
Gyroscope; Magnet; Navigation;
North Pole

 ## COMPOSER

A man or woman who makes up music is a composer. If you make up a little melody to hum you are composing a tune. If you play some notes on the piano just for fun, you are beginning to compose. If you like the sounds you have made, you can write them down so that you can play them again.

Composers use *tones,* or sounds, to write music. They combine them in different ways, using one at a time or many tones together. They use *rhythm,* so that some sounds move quickly while others last longer. Composers can use human voices as well as many musical instruments, combining them to make interesting tones. They may combine all the instruments and voices into a large work for chorus and orchestra. Or they may want just the piano or the violin for a piece of music. They are then writing a *solo* for that instrument.

Some composers can make up music without studying composition, but most people have to learn to use sounds and rhythms that go into music. They study how different tones go together in the system of scales and keys (harmony). They learn to play the piano and perhaps other musical instruments. They learn what notes men or women can sing. When composers know these things, they are able to use them in their own way to create music which sounds, when it is played, just as they "hear" it in their minds.

Composers use special paper ruled for *musical notation,* the written language of music. They write symbols for notes on the lines and spaces. Each note shows which sound is to be played and for how long. There are also symbols for "rests" of various lengths at points where the composer wants no sound at all. Composers show what key or *tonality* the piece

Stephen Foster was one of America's best-loved songwriters—he wrote favorites such as "Swanee River," "Oh! Susanna," and "My Old Kentucky Home." He never had any music lessons, but by the age of 6 he had taught himself to play the clarinet. Foster wrote more than 200 songs, many of which were sung by people all over the world, but he died in poverty in New York City in 1860.

▲ **The great composer, Franz Joseph Haydn.**

will be played in. They then add signs telling whether the music is to be loud or soft, whether it is to slow down or speed up, and many other things. This collection of symbols is called a *music manuscript* or *score*.

The manuscripts of famous composers are very valuable. They are often kept in libraries and museums

▼ The composer Beethoven went to Vienna in 1787 and played for Mozart.

▲ Karlheinz Stockhausen is a modern composer. His music includes electronic sounds.

where music students may study them. Some composers today use a music typewriter, called a *music-writer,* instead of drawing notes by hand.

Some Famous Composers

Music goes back to very ancient times, but little is known about actual pieces of music written before the 1200s and 1300s. Some of the earliest known composers wrote music for religious services. *Musicologists*, students who study music history, have been able to learn about many of the composers who have written music since that time.

Many countries have had great composers whose music became internationally known. Johann Sebastian Bach, Ludwig van Beethoven, Johannes Brahms, Felix Mendelssohn, Robert Schumann, and Richard Wagner were from Germany. Franz Joseph Haydn, Wolfgang Amadeus Mozart, Franz Schubert, and Johann Strauss were from Austria. Sergei Prokofiev, Sergei Rachmaninoff, Igor Stravinsky, and Peter I. Tchaikovsky were Russian. Frédéric Chopin was Polish. George Frederick Handel was a German who worked in England. Guiseppe Verdi was Italian. Franz Liszt of Hungary, Edvard Grieg of Norway, and Claude Debussy of France studied and composed in many European countries.

America has also produced many famous composers, including Stephen Foster, John Philip Sousa, George and Ira Gershwin, George M. Cohan, Irving Berlin, Aaron Copland, Richard Rogers, Oscar Hammerstein, and Leonard Bernstein. You may read about these composers in this encyclopedia. Today, many younger composers are developing electronic music and are exploring new ways of writing music. Some composers have created new and different styles of music. Others are

LEARN BY DOING

Have you ever wanted to compose a song? One way to begin is by taking a favorite poem and thinking up music to go with the words. If you know how to play a musical instrument, you probably know how to write down the song on music paper. If you have a tape recorder, you can sing or whistle the tune that you have made up in your head and record it on tape. Someone else (perhaps your music teacher) could then help you write out your song by playing back the tape recording.

famous because they brought one style to its highest development.

Many composers write music in each century. Some become famous while they are alive but are forgotten later. Sometimes the music is appreciated only after the composer dies. The music of some composers is widely played and praised, and then forgotten. Long afterward it may be discovered again and become popular. For example, Bach's music was forgotten by most people for nearly a hundred years after his death. Interest in his work was revived in the 1800s.

▶▶▶▶ **FIND OUT MORE** ◀◀◀◀
Art; Electronic Music; Music; Opera
For individual composers see Index.

COMPOSITION

In writing, *composition* means "to put a story down on paper." Perhaps in the first and second grades, you and your classmates wrote a story together in reading class. The teacher really did the writing on a huge sheet of paper in front of the class. You all told her what words to use, and she printed them on the paper. It is surprising what a good story a class of students can write together.

Now you write compositions by yourself. Instead of having the class give you ideas, you supply the ideas out of your head. This is easy if you write about a subject you like. Before you start to write, think about something you really like—swimming, camping, Little League baseball, or friends in the playground, for instance. Choose one subject. Remember, you want to interest the reader, so, you, the writer must be interested in the subject.

To tell your story, you must have a form that holds it together. There must be a beginning, a middle, and an end. If you think of a good way to start your story, you are well on your way. Sometimes the middle part is the

hardest. To fill out the body of the composition, you need a lot of details or facts about your subject. If you are writing about swimming, for instance, tell about how far you can swim, what strokes you can do, and what you like best about swimming.

Move on to finish your composition by writing the end. The end should tie together the major ideas of your story.

Your story should have some sequence—the sentences should follow one another in an order that makes sense. You can help show sequence by using paragraphs. Start a new paragraph for each new idea. The number of paragraphs you have depends on how much you have to say.

Do remember that although writing is like talk written down, you have much more time to plan exactly what you want to say, and how you want to say it. Try writing a composition today.

▶▶▶▶ **FIND OUT MORE** ◀◀◀◀
Grammar; Language Arts;
Letter Writing; Punctuation; Spelling

COMPOUND

SEE CHEMISTRY

COMPUTER

How long would it take you to add together 1+2+3+4+5 and so on up to 1,000? Even if you worked quickly, it would take you a long time to get the answer (500,500). Besides, you would have to do each of the thousand additions correctly or you would wind up with the wrong answer after all that hard work.

With a home computer, you would need about a minute to key in the program or instructions it needs. The computer would then do the additions in about one second. And it would always be right.

GLOSSARY OF TERMS

Binary code The code of 0's and 1's that makes up computer "language."

Digital Using numbers; digital chips work with numerical quantities only.

Disk drive An information storage unit used to feed a program or information into a computer from a magnetic disk.

Hard drive Internal information storage unit.

Hardware Everything you can see and touch on a microcomputer.

Microchip Tiny piece of silicon that holds the electronic circuits in a computer.

Modem Equipment that turns computer signals into telephone signals and back again.

Monitor A display unit; a screen, as on a TV set, for displaying the output of a computer.

Program Software instructions that tell a computer how to solve a problem.

Software The programs that tell a computer what to do.

Transistor An electronic component that can be used as a switch or an amplifier; the principal component of microelectronic circuits.

It seems almost impossible that tiny chips, such as the one in the center of the panel, can do the work of the enormous machines, shown below.

ENIAC, completed in 1946, was the first really electronic machine. It had 18,000 vacuum tubes that kept burning out at an alarming rate.

To "compute" means to count or to figure. A computer is a machine that solves problems many times faster than a person can. A computer does not think, so a person must give it information, supply instructions on how to solve the problem, and tell in what form the answer is to be given.

Computers can answer many kinds of problems, and also store and handle information. They have played a most important role in the space program and in weather forecasting, where answers are needed quickly. If these answers had to be worked out by hand, they would not be ready for days or weeks.

Libraries, schools, hospitals, police, and businesses use computers to save many hours of searching through files. Today, when you give a librarian your topic for a science project, you will probably get a list of useful books in seconds! Doctors use computers to keep records on patients and provide up-to-date information on medicines and their effects on certain diseases. Computers can even help doctors find the cause of an illness.

At a space center, computers stop the countdown for a space launch if a part is not working right. The computer keeps the spacecraft on the correct flight path by constantly controlling its speed and direction.

Computers can also be programmed to write and perform music, check income tax, create pictures, and play games of all kinds, especially chess.

The First Computer

Charles Babbage (1792–1871), an Englishman, was the first to think of a machine that could be given information and instructions to solve arithmetic problems. He worked on it for almost 38 years, but at that time no one could make the complex parts needed for his computer.

It was not until electronics developed that a computer could be made. (You can read more about electronics in volume 7 of this library.) The first electronic computer was a British computer called COLOSSUS, which was invented in 1943. It was built during World War II to crack enemy coded messages. However, it could not do any other task. The first general-purpose computer was an American computer called ENIAC, completed in 1946.

These early computers, which contained thousands of glass, light-bulb shaped vacuum tubes, were massive machines that took up large rooms. Computers became smaller and more powerful with the development of the *transistor,* which replaced vacuum tubes, and the *microchip,* which contains thousands of microscopic transistors linked together. A home computer today is far more powerful than the first giant computers.

How a Computer Works

A computer is a digital machine, which means that it does everything by numbers. It changes all the information it is given, including words, into code numbers called *binary code.* The code makes electric signals that move along the wires in the computer and in and out of its microchips and other parts called *components.*

These components handle the code

signals in various ways. They can add two numbers together or compare two numbers to see if they are the same, for example, producing a result in the form of another code signal. They do these operations very quickly and the signals move at very high speed. Other components store the signals until they are needed. When the final result is produced, the computer changes the code signal into a form we can understand, such as words or numbers.

To operate, a computer has to follow a set of instructions that "tell" it how to perform a particular task. The set of instructions is called a computer *program*. The program is fed into the computer, where it is stored as a sequence of electric code signals. These code signals make the computer's components perform the correct sequence of operations to produce the result.

Computer Hardware

The *hardware* of a computer system is the actual machinery—the computer itself and other equipment to which it is connected. The whole system has four basic parts, or units: the input, processor, memory and output units. In microcomputers, which are small computers like those used at home and in offices, these units may all be linked together within one case. In minicomputers, mainframes, and supercomputers (large computers used in businesses) the units may be separate pieces that are connected together.

The *input* unit is used to feed information into the computer or to control the computer as it operates. The keyboard is an important input unit; you use it to "type" in words and numbers and to press special keys that make things happen. Other input units include the mouse, joystick, and light pen, which are hand-operated controls. With a pressure-sensitive pen, you can write on the screen of a

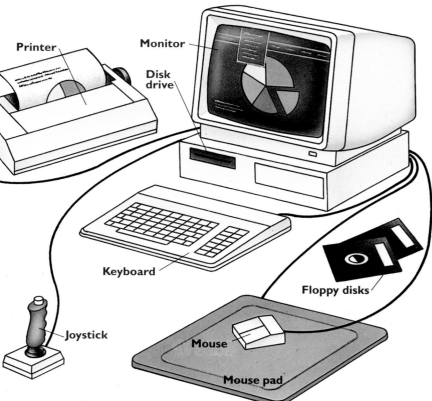

Printer · **Monitor** · **Disk drive** · **Keyboard** · **Joystick** · **Mouse** · **Mouse pad** · **Floppy disks**

▲ Some of the devices that can be used to input information into a computer. They include a joystick, often used when playing games; a mouse; and a keyboard. Disks store information.

computer just like on paper. A voice recognition unit can respond to certain patterns of speech. You speak into it to give the computer information and commands.

The *memory* unit gives the computer the instructions that it needs. It also stores the information that comes from the input unit. There are several different kinds of memory units. The ROM (read-only memory) is a microchip (CD-ROM is a compact disc) inside the computer that contains *permanent* programs of instructions enabling the computer to work. The RAM (random-access memory) is another chip that stores programs and information for only as long as they are needed. New programs and information can be fed into RAM whenever required so that the computer can perform different tasks.

These programs and information can be stored inside the computer on a hard drive or outside the computer on a disk called a floppy. A unit such as a disk drive is used to feed the required program and information from the floppy disk into the computer.

The *processor* unit is the brain of

▲ **You can even play a game of chess with a computer. A special program tells the computer what moves to make and the memory keeps a record of all the moves made.**

Computer scientists today are working toward the ultra-intelligent machine—a machine that can think and learn from its own experience, just as we do. Many people think that sometime during the 21st century there will be computers that can work out problems and discover scientific laws better than humans can. In business, computers will run whole industries. At chess, they will beat all the Grand Masters. But it is doubtful whether a computer will ever write a play as well as Shakespeare did or compose a sonata as beautiful as those of Mozart.

the computer. It follows the program instructions and takes the information from the memory or input units to produce a result. This result goes to the *output* unit, called a monitor or display screen. It looks like a television screen that displays words, numbers, and pictures. Other output units include a computer printer, a plotter that draws pictures, a speech synthesizer that talks, and a robot arm that moves. There is also a *modem*, which can send the output signals along telephone wires to a modem at the other end. This serves as an input unit for a computer at that end.

Computer Software

The *software* of a computer consists of the various programs that make the computer do different things. The programs come on disks that are loaded into the computer. Different kinds of software can turn the computer into a word processor, spreadsheet, or database, which are common business uses for computers. There are also games and music software for entertainment, and educational software that makes the computer useful as a teaching aid. Hand-held computer games have become very popular.

Computer programmers write the programs that are sold as software. They work at the keyboard of a computer and feed in the various instructions. The computer itself works with code signals, which are not easily handled by the programmer. He or she, therefore, uses a "programming language" to write the program. The language often has English words to make it easy for the programmer to write and understand the program. Another program called a compiler, or interpreter, in the memory translates the language instructions into code signals.

▶ ▶ ▶ ▶ **FIND OUT MORE** ◀ ◀ ◀ ◀
Automation; Babbage, Charles; Bardeen, John; Binary System; Calculator; Compact Disc; Electronics

CONCRETE

All kinds of structures—houses, skyscrapers, bridges, dams, oil rigs, and more—can be built of concrete. Many buildings contain concrete beams and slabs in the walls and floors, and some are constructed on top of huge blocks of concrete buried in the ground to provide strong foundations. Roads are often made of layers of concrete beneath a surface of tar and gravel.

The reason that concrete can be used in so many different ways is that it can be formed into any shape required, yet is very strong. A whole arch or dome, for example, can be made in one piece using concrete. Large panels and slabs of concrete can be made in a factory and then taken to the building site and fixed together.

Many of the modern buildings and structures in towns and cities are made of concrete, unlike older houses built of brick or stone. However, concrete is not a new building material. It was invented in ancient times. The

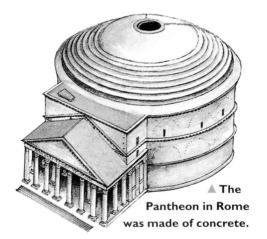

▲ **The Pantheon in Rome was made of concrete.**

Romans used concrete to build aqueducts and even the Colosseum.

Concrete is made by mixing sand, cement, and water together with small stones such as gravel or crushed rock. The wet concrete is poured into a mold and sets hard in the shape of the mold. *Cement* is made by burning a mixture of limestone or chalk and clay in a kiln, and then crushing it into

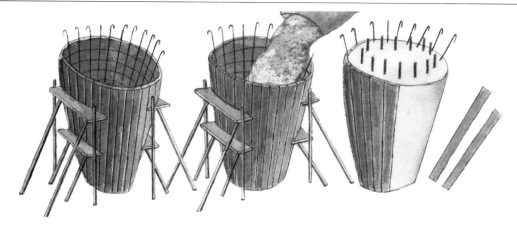

◀ Concrete can be poured into a mold of any shape. Today, concrete in a building's structure is almost always reinforced by the addition of thin steel rods.

powder. When water is added, cement sets hard. In concrete, the cement binds the sand and stones together to produce a hard material.

Concrete, however, is not very strong when used alone. It tends to crack if subjected to heavy loads. To increase its strength, it is reinforced by putting steel rods in the concrete to take the strain. Pre-stressed concrete contains steel bars that squeeze or compress the concrete, making it much stronger.

▶ ▶ ▶ **FIND OUT MORE** ◀ ◀ ◀
Building Material; Construction

CONDENSATION

SEE WATER CYCLE

CONDUCTION

SEE HEAT AND COLD

CONFEDERATE STATES OF AMERICA

A group of Southern states withdrew from the United States in December of 1860 and early in 1861. These states joined together after Abraham Lincoln was elected President of the United States in 1860. Many people in these states disagreed strongly with Lincoln's ideas and believed he would make slavery illegal. They formed their

own country, named the Confederate States of America.

Six states—South Carolina, Mississippi, Florida, Alabama, Georgia, and Louisiana—originally formed the Confederacy. Representatives from each of the states held a meeting in Montgomery, Alabama, early in 1861. They chose Montgomery as the capital of the Confederacy. They elected Jefferson Davis as president. Alexander Hamilton Stephens of Georgia was elected vice-president. Davis chose six advisers for his cabinet. The representatives then drew up a constitution. They established an elected congress, made up of representatives from the states as well as the nonvoting members of the cabinet. The president and vice-president had six year terms of office. They issued their own money. A permanent army was put under the control of the government. Slavery was declared legal.

The North refused to allow the secession of the Confederate States, and the Civil War broke out in April 1861. Texas, Virginia, Arkansas,

▼ The Confederate States of America. The first states to join were South Carolina, Alabama, Florida, Georgia, Louisiana, and Mississippi, in February 1861.

▶ Jefferson Davis announced the secession of the South from the Union in Montgomery, Alabama, the first Confederate capital. Shortly after, the Civil War began.

THE FIRST MEMBERS OF THE CONFEDERATE CABINET

President:
Jefferson Davis
Vice President:
Alexander H. Stephens
Secretary of State:
Robert Toombs
Secretary of the Treasury:
Christopher Memminger
Secretary of War:
Leroy P. Walker
Secretary of the Navy:
Stephen R. Mallory
Postmaster General:
John H. Reagan
Attorney General:
Judah P. Benjamin

▶ The emblem of the Confederation of Canada. Canada is a member of the Commonwealth of Nations.

North Carolina, and Tennessee joined the Confederacy later that year, and the capital was moved to Richmond, Virginia. The counties of northwestern Virginia wanted to remain loyal to the union. They created their own new state, West Virginia, in 1863.

The Confederates had little money to pay for the war and very few soldiers to fight it. Large taxes were levied, and the people gave generously. But the Confederates were soon in serious financial trouble. They were unable to get enough aid from the foreign countries—France, Britain, the Netherlands, Spain, and Brazil—who agreed to trade with them. Moreover, many of their ships were blockaded by the Union navy. The South won several battles under General Robert E. Lee's command, but after two years, the wealthy, industrial North began to win the war. The Confederacy not only lacked the needed supplies, but its leaders disagreed over how the war should be fought. In April 1865, Davis and his cabinet were forced to escape from Richmond, which was under attack by Northern armies. Later that month, the Confederate States of America collapsed and the war was over.

▶▶▶ **FIND OUT MORE** ◀◀◀
Civil War; Davis, Jefferson; Lincoln, Abraham; Slavery; West Virginia

CONFEDERATION OF CANADA

Like the United States, Canada has a *federal* system of government. Its ten provinces and two territories have some powers of their own, but national decisions are made by the central government in Ottawa. This close union of provinces and territories is called a *confederation.*

But there are important differences between the Canadian and American systems of government. For example, the Canadian *federal* (central) government has more powers than the U.S. federal government. And there is no Canadian president. Instead there is a prime *minister* who leads the party with the most seats in the Canadian *parliament.*

The Confederation of Canada was established in the 1860s. Until that time there were seven separate British colonies north of the United States. Many Canadians were the descendants of Loyalists who had fled the United States during the Revolutionary War. They were happy to keep their ties with Britain. And they already had a form of self-government. But they also saw the need to unite.

At a meeting in Charlottetown, Prince Edward Island, in 1864, Canadian leaders agreed to form a strong union, or confederation. Those present at this meeting are known as the *Fathers of Confederation.* Britain approved the plans for the Confederation of Canada. On July 1, 1867, the British Parliament passed the British North America Act, creating the Dominion of Canada. This British Act served as Canada's constitution until 1982, when it was transferred back to Canada.

▶▶▶ **FIND OUT MORE** ◀◀◀
Canada; Fathers of Confederation; Macdonald, John A.; Revolutionary War

CONFUCIUS
(about 551–479 B.C.)

Confucius was a great Chinese philosopher. He was born in what is now the province of Shandong, China. His family was very poor. When Confucius was only three, his father died. His mother did her best to see he got a good education. When he was 21, students began to come to listen to him.

Confucius taught that men should be honest, loyal, thoughtful toward others, and obedient. He said that life has five main relationships. These are between ruler and subject, father and son, elder and younger brother, husband and wife, and friend and friend. Each of these relationships includes duties and responsibilities that should be carried out as well as possible. Each person must do his duty to the other. The two most important ways to make these relationships work, he said, were *jen* (love) and *li* (manners or etiquette). Confucius had many wise sayings. The most familiar of all was "What you do not wish done to yourself, do not do to others." Jesus Christ taught this philosophy—the Golden Rule—500 years later.

When Confucius was 52, he was made governor of his state. It is said that he did such a good job of ruling it that a neighboring governor became jealous, so Confucius gave up his post. He spent the next 13 years searching for a prince who would listen to his ideas, so that he could demonstrate the principles of good government. But China was governed by many dishonest leaders in those days.

Confucius died almost unknown, but his ideas have since come to be followed by millions of people. He taught a way of looking at life and

the universe, not a religion. But his teachings slowly became mixed with old Chinese customs to form a religion. Confucianism has played an important part in the culture and history of China, Korea, and Japan.

▶▶▶▶ FIND OUT MORE ◀◀◀◀
China; Philosophy; Religion

CONGO

The People's Republic of the Congo is a Central African nation that used to be called Congo (Brazzaville). Brazzaville is the name of the country's capital. This name was used because the country's neighbor, Zaire, was until 1971 also called the Congo. Congo (Brazzaville) was a French colony until it received independence in 1960.

Congo is approximately twice the size of Washington state. It is bordered on the west by Gabon, on the north by Cameroon and the Central

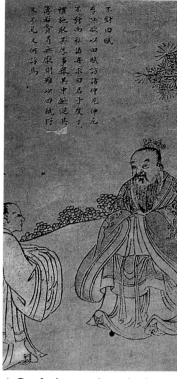
▲ Confucius was born in the 6th century B.C. in China.

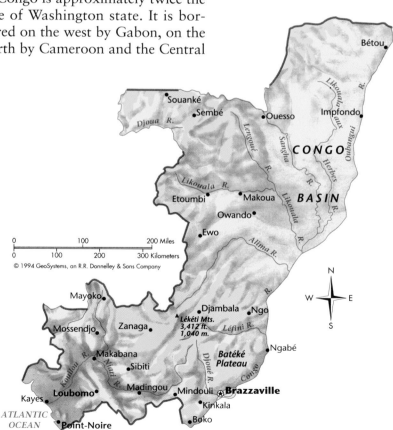

CONGO

Capital city
Brazzaville (596,000 people)

Area
132,047 square miles (342,000 sq. km)

Population
2,326,000 people

Government
Republic

Natural resources
Lumber, oil

Export products
Oil, lumber, fertilizers, coffee, cocoa

Unit of money
Franc of the African Financial Community

Official language
French

▲ The badge of members of the U.S. Congress, the law-making branch of the federal government.

African Republic, and on the east and south by Zaire. The Atlantic Ocean forms the southwestern boundary. The equator runs through the middle of the country.

Congo has three geographical regions. The narrow coastal plain extends 40 miles (64 km) inland. Highlands form the central part of the country. In the north lies the basin of the Congo River. This river, called the Zaire River in Zaire, separates Congo from Zaire. It is a major transportation route.

Congo has a tropical climate. Rain falls throughout the year in most of the country. The coastal plain of Congo is cooler and drier than the rest of the land.

Over one-half of the Congolese live by raising only the crops they need for their own use. Others also raise crops that can be exported, such as peanuts, coffee, cocoa, palm kernels, and tobacco. Some people earn a living by fishing and lumbering.

Congo has little industry. The waterfalls on several rivers may someday be used for hydroelectric power, however. Oil is now by far the leading export. Lead, gold, and diamonds are also mined.

The Congolese belong to several ethnic and language groups. Almost half of the people are members of the Bakongo group. Others belong to the Bateke, M'Bochi, and Sangha. Many of them speak French, the nation's official language, in addition to their local languages.

The country is a transport hub of central Africa. The Congo River system and the Congo-Ocean Railroad connect inland areas with Pointe-Noire, the country's main seaport.

▶▶▶▶ **FIND OUT MORE** ◀◀◀◀
Africa; Zaire River

CONGO RIVER

SEE ZAIRE RIVER

CONGRESS, UNITED STATES

"All legislative powers herein granted shall be vested in a Congress of the United States, which shall consist of a Senate and a House of Representatives." These words establish the U.S. Congress for the purpose of making the nation's laws.

The government of the United States is divided into three branches so that no one person or group can acquire too much power. This is called the "check and balance" system of government. Each branch has specific powers to *check* (stop) the others if one tries to become too powerful. The powers of each branch balance the powers of the other two branches.

The President of the United States and the people who work with him form the *executive* branch of the government. The Supreme Court and the federal court system form the *judicial* branch of the government. Congress makes up the *legislative* branch of the government. This branch is called legislative because "to legislate" means "to make laws," and making laws is the main job of Congress. The English word *congress* comes from a Latin word meaning "come together." When the U.S. Congress holds a session, members of Congress meet in the Capitol building in Washington, D.C.

The United States Congress is a *bicameral* legislature. This means that it has two houses (parts), the *Senate* and the *House of Representatives*. The powers of Congress are divided between these two houses. This is another example of the check and balance system. The Senate and the House of Representatives must work together to make new laws.

The House of Representatives
The House of Representatives has been called the *lower house* of Congress, and the Senate has been called

HOW A BILL BECOMES LAW

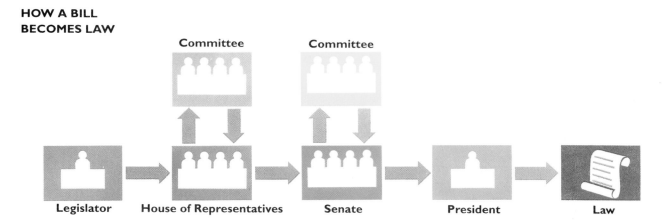

the *upper house*. These names were chosen when Congress was first set up. The House of Representatives at that time was less powerful than the Senate. Now both houses are about equal in power.

Members of the House of Representatives are called *representatives* because they represent the people who elect them. They are also called *congressmen* or *congresswomen*. A representative is elected for a two-year term, usually by people of a particular area in his or her home state. Each area, called a *congressional district*, is set by the legislature of each state according to population. A representative may be reelected by the people of the district every two years. If they are not satisfied with the job being done, they elect someone else. The House is said to be the chamber closest to the people, because voters express their opinion every two years.

The first meeting of the House was held in 1789 with 65 representatives. The number of representatives increased steadily until 1911. The House then decided that adding more members would be impractical, so the number of representatives was set at 435. The number of people represented by each representative is constantly growing. The number of congressional districts in each state depends on the number of people in that state, but each state has

at least one. Although not a state, Washington, D.C. has one non-voting representative.

The number of congressional districts in each state is adjusted after each *census* (a count of the population taken every ten years) to ensure that every state has its fair share of representatives.

The leader of the House of Representatives is called the *Speaker of the House*. The Speaker is chosen at the beginning of each new Congress by representatives of the political party that elects the majority of congressmen. If anything happens to the President and Vice President, the Speaker becomes President. The members hold separate meetings, by party, to choose four other leaders: the House Majority Leader and the Majority Whip and the House Minority Leader and the Minority Whip. Majority and minority leaders, or *floor leaders*, as they are often called, try to keep the lawmaking process running smoothly. The whips make sure that all the representatives are present for important votes.

The House of Representatives has many special powers. It is allowed to *impeach* (bring charges against) the President or other federal officials if the representatives think they are guilty of wrongdoing. The House also has the power to introduce *bills* (proposals for new laws) concerning *revenue* (money that the government

▲ All bills must be passed by both houses of Congress and signed by the President before becoming law. A bill vetoed (not signed) by the President can still become law if it is passed a second time by a two-thirds vote of both chambers.

Article 1 of the United States Constitution tells us who shall or shall not sit in Congress:
A Representative must have reached the age of 25 and been a citizen of the United States for seven years. A Representative must also be an inhabitant of the state from which he or she is elected.
A Senator must be 30 years of age and must have been a United States citizen for nine years. A Senator must also be an inhabitant of the state in which he or she is chosen.
The President has to be a natural-born citizen of the United States. He or she must be at least 35 years of age and must have been a U.S. resident for at least 14 years.

▲ The U.S. House of Representatives has 435 members. The public is allowed to watch the House in session from the balcony.

collects from taxes and other sources). The Senate must approve any new revenue bill after the House passes it, but only the House can begin the process of making a new revenue law. The House forms committees that study problems and hold hearings to help in deciding whether a new idea should become a law. Each committee specializes in certain subjects, such as agriculture or education.

The Senate

Members of the Senate are called *senators*. Two senators are elected from each state, whether it is large or small. All the voters in a state elect that state's senators, who serve for six years. The United States now has 50 states, so Congress has 100 senators. Not all senators run for election at the same time. Instead, one-third of the Senate is elected every two years. The Vice-President of the United States presides over the Senate. When the Vice-President is elsewhere, a senator called the *president pro tempore* ("temporary president") presides. He or she is elected by the other senators.

Like the House, the Senate has some special powers. The Senate must *ratify* (approve) all treaties with foreign governments. If the President or some other official is impeached by the House, the Senate becomes a court. Whoever is impeached must

stand trial before the Senate. If found guilty, that person is removed from office. The Senate must also *confirm* (approve) the President's choices for Cabinet members and Supreme Court justices. Like the House, the Senate forms committees to help in its work. One of the most important committees is the one on foreign affairs. Most of the real work of Congress is done "in committee." This is why the Senate and House are often deserted, even when Congress is in session.

Congress has other powers that both houses share. Only Congress can declare war or raise and support an army and navy. Congress can set up federal courts, make laws regulating certain kinds of business, and borrow money for the government. It can provide money to help foreign nations in need, to build weapons for national defense, to pay for medical research, and to build highways. Congress can propose amendments to the Constitution of the United States and decide when to admit new states into the Union.

Congress ran the city of Washington from 1878 to 1974, when home rule was enacted.

How Congress Makes Laws

Any member of either house may start the process of making a law, except for a bill concerning revenue, which must begin in the lower house. Suppose a member of the House of Representatives wants to pass a new law that will provide money for a school health program. He or she begins by "drafting" a bill. This means writing a suggestion for a new law in legal language for other representatives to read and think about. This bill is put into the "hopper," a box for new bills on the desk of the clerk of the House of Representatives.

The clerk sends the bill to a committee for study. In this case, the clerk would probably send the bill to the House Education and Labor Committee because it is about money for schools. The members of the committee read the bill. They may hold hearings, meetings at which experts come to Congress to discuss the bill. The experts might include teachers, school principals, parents, doctors, and nurses. The committee members listen and think. If they decide the bill is a good one, they "report it out to the floor"—they present the bill to all the other members of the House. On the "floor" of the House, the other representatives discuss the bill. All those who want to speak about the bill have a chance to do so. The House then votes on it. The bill is sent to the Senate if the majority of the House passes it.

The bill is now studied by a Senate committee. New hearings are held. Experts come again to give their opinions of the bill. Afterwards the bill is debated on the "floor" of the Senate. If most senators vote for the bill, it is sent to the President.

The President has the power to approve or disapprove a bill. A bill signed by the President becomes law. The President's power to disapprove of a bill is called the *veto power*. If the President vetoes the bill, it is sent back to Congress. The members of both houses think about the bill some more. They may change the bill to try to gain the President's approval. If they do not agree with the President, they can again vote in favor of the bill. A bill becomes a law even though the President has vetoed it if two-thirds of the members of each house vote in favor of it. This is called "overriding" the veto.

▶▶▶▶FIND OUT MORE◀◀◀◀
Capitol, United States; Constitution, United States; Court System; Presidency; Supreme Court; United States Government

CONIFER

The world's oldest, tallest, and heaviest living things are *conifers*—cone-bearing trees. So are the trees that grow at the highest places: at the timberline among mountains, and the trees growing in the coldest places: at the treeline in the snowy wastes of the Arctic region. Nearly all the paper and three-fourths of the world's lumber come from conifers.

The greatest assortment of conifers in the whole world grows in the western United States. But the huge redwood, the 3,000-year-old sequoia, the beautiful Monterey pine, and the rare pygmy cypress are all in danger of becoming extinct, mainly because of the action of humans. Many large sequoia are now protected by the U.S. Government.

Nearly 500 kinds of conifers exist grouped in seven different families. The pine is probably the best known. Spruces, hemlocks, cedars, and firs are other familiar coniferous trees.

Conifers are easy to recognize by their leaves. The leaves of many conifers are not broad and flat, like an oak leaf, but long, slim, and pointed. They are thus called "needles." Pine needles grow out from the branch in bunches of two to five, depending on the type of pine tree. Some needles grow 9 inches (23 cm) long. Other kinds of conifers have scaly leaves. Almost all conifers are *evergreens*, trees whose branches are never bare of leaves. The leaves of many coniferous trees remain on the branches for several years before they are replaced.

▲ The cones of a sitka spruce, a type of conifer.

The oldest conifer and also the world's oldest living thing is a bristlecone pine growing on Wheeler Peak in east Nevada. This ancient tree is probably 4,900 years old, having been alive for over 2,900 years before the birth of Christ.

▼ The cone of the giant sequoia.

◀ A conifer, the redwood, is the tallest tree in the world. One in California was over 375 feet (112 m) tall.

▼ **Cone**

▲ **Monterey pine**

▼ **Cone**

▲ **Douglas fir**

▼ **Unripe Cone**

▲ **Western hemlock**

Conifers have special seeds, too. The seeds of other trees are enclosed in a hard or fleshy fruit. The seeds of an apple tree, for example, are in the center of the fruit. Coniferous trees have seeds that are not covered. Instead they are carried on the upper surfaces of the scales that make up the cone. Some trees have seedcones that ripen in a year, but other varieties take two years to develop fully. Botanists classify conifers as *gymnosperms*, or naked, seeded trees. All other trees are *angiosperms*, or trees with covered seeds.

The Pines

The pines may be the conifer family you know best. The *white pine* grows all across the northern United States. In colonial days, the British made a law that the big white pines, 60 feet (18 m) high, must be saved for masts for ships of the British navy. Pines are useful in the timber and paper industries. In southern states, turpentine is produced from pine trees. In the eastern states, important pine trees are *longleaf* and *loblolly*. The *lodgepole* and *ponderosa* pines are important in the West. In the Southwest, there is the *pinyon* pine, which produces delicious pine nuts.

Some pines grow as high as 240 feet (73 m). They also live very long lives. Experts say that more than a dozen *bristlecone* pines have survived for over 4,000 years in the White Mountains of California.

The *Douglas fir* of the northwestern mountains is not a true fir, but a pine closely related to the hemlock. It is among our largest trees, sometimes reaching 200 feet (60 m) in height, although the average is closer to 100 feet (30 m). Millions of young Douglas firs are cut each year.

Hemlocks, also part of the pine family, are very common in the mountains of the East and Northwest. They grow best in cool, damp climates. Hemlocks reach heights of 60–100

feet (18–30 m) and are important in the timber industry. Four different types are found in the United States. They are the eastern, Carolina, mountain, and western hemlock. The bark of the hemlock is rich in *tannin*, used in tanning leather.

Balsam fir is a very popular Christmas pine. It grows in New England, around the Great Lakes, and in Canada. Blisters on the bark of the balsam produce a resin. The cement made from this resin makes a useful transparent cement. Balsam firs provide shelter for wildlife. Birds feed on the seeds and deer and rabbits eat the bark and young branches.

Birds and animals also feed on *spruce*, another kind of pine. Spruce trees are harvested for lumber for the building industry and for pulpwood, used in making paper. The *red spruce*, *white spruce*, and *black spruce* grow in the cool forests of the eastern mountains. *Blue spruce* is one of the western varieties. The *Norway spruce*, brought here from Europe, is another popular tree.

Amber comes from pine trees. It is the resin from ancient pine trees that fell to the ground and hardened over millions of years.

Other Conifer Families

The *araucarians* are one conifer family of which few species have survived. We know that this family is very old. The trees that turned to stone in the Petrified Forest of Arizona are araucarians. Some of those ancient trunks are 200 feet (60 m) long.

Most surviving araucarians are found in the Southern Hemisphere. One you may know is the *Norfolk Island "pine."* It is often grown in pots as a house plant in northern climates, although it comes from a warm place in New Zealand. The *monkey-puzzle tree* of Chile has hard, spiky needles and branches that interlock.

The hugest trees in the world belong to the *bald cypress* family. The *dawn redwood* belongs to this group, along with the *giant sequoia* and the *"big cypress"* of Mexico. One sequoia, called General Sherman, is 272 feet (83 m) tall and 101½ feet (31 m) around the base. The "big cypress" in Santa Maria del Tule, Mexico, has a base circumference of 112 feet (34 m). Either of these trees—and others in this family nearly as big—contains enough wood to build a dozen houses, with plenty left over. The seed of the *redwood*, in a cone an inch (2.5 cm) long, is very tiny.

The *cypress* family includes the many kinds of *juniper*. The beautiful *arborvitae*, often used as hedges, also belongs to this family. The *red cedar* also is a cypress.

The *yews* are another conifer family. Soldiers of William the Conqueror's time knew that wood from the *English yew* made the best bows. Other species of yew grow as small trees or shrubs with handsome needles. The *Canada yew* grows as shrubbery in the United States.

The *podocarps* are a strange conifer family. Most grow in remote places in the Southern Hemisphere. Australia has a *blackpine* in this family, and New Zealand a brown timber which the Maori called *miro-miro*. Some podocarps would hardly be recognized as conifers, except that they produce cones. The tiniest conifer of all is a podocarp—

▲ Giant sequoias are large conifers. Their bark is reddish brown, thick, fibrous, and so soft it can be punched without hurting your fist.

the New Zealand *pygmy pine*. This tree grows cones when it is only three inches (7.6 cm) tall.

The *phylloclads* of Tasmania, New Zealand, and the South Pacific islands shed their tiny leaves. They are one exception to the general rule that a conifer is evergreen and has needles.

▶▶▶▶ **FIND OUT MORE** ◀◀◀◀
Amber; Evergreen Tree; Forest Fire; Forestry; Lumber and Lumbering; Paper; Tree

CONJUNCTION

SEE PARTS OF SPEECH

CONNECTICUT

In area, Connecticut is a very small state. Only Delaware and Rhode Island are smaller. But in its contributions to the United States, Connecticut is very large indeed.

Nautilus, the world's first atomic-powered submarine—and many other submarines, too—was built in the huge shipyard at Groton. Until about 100 years ago, Connecticut's ship builders turned out sturdy sailing ships and whalers. Connecticut has been a leading manufacturing state—not only of submarines, but of helicopters, airplane engines, machine tools, and ball and roller bearings. Other important goods made in the state are electrical products such as switches, outlets, and appliances; hardware such as nuts,

Spiky leaves

▲ A monkey-puzzle tree

▲ The berries of a common juniper

▼ Yew tree with berrylike cones

▲ The State Capitol building in Hartford, Connecticut.

One of Connecticut's nicknames is the Nutmeg State. This name comes from a story told about early Connecticut traders. People say that they made wooden nutmegs and sold them as real ones: this shows how valuable nutmegs once were.

▼ There are many attractive buildings in Connecticut like this white, wood-framed house.

bolts, valves, and pipes; clothing; firearms; chemicals; plastics; optical instruments; pharmaceuticals; and surgical instruments.

Many other products such as silverware, clocks and thread were once manufactured in Connecticut, too. However, factories where these products were made have closed because of competition from foreign companies, who can make the same products for less money.

The northeastern region of the United States is called New England. Connecticut is the southernmost New England state. All this manufacturing would be a surprise to a Connecticut Yankee who lived 150 years ago. (A Yankee is a New Englander.) Until the 1850s, almost all the people of Connecticut were farmers. But in 50 years, the scene in the state changed from one of quiet farms to one of busy factories. You will see how all of this came to happen after you read about the area and the people of the state of Connecticut.

The Land

Connecticut is bordered on the west by New York State, on the north by Massachusetts, and on the east by Rhode Island. The southern side is coastline, where the waves of Long Island Sound splash the shore. Long Island Sound is an arm of the Atlantic Ocean. It lies between the mainland of Connecticut and Long Island, part of New York State.

The southwest corner of Connecticut lies very close to New York City. Highways and railroads link the cities of Stamford, Bridgeport and the university city of New Haven with New York. Thousands of people who work in New York City live in Connecticut. They travel (commute) to work each day by car or by train.

The Connecticut River, which begins in northern New Hampshire and is 407 miles (656 km) long, flows south through the center of the state into Long Island Sound. Small ships can sail up the river as far as Hartford. Farther north, at Windsor Locks, water tumbling from one level to another provides power, and the broad river valley is good for farming.

Sixty percent of Connecticut is forested. Its green, rolling hills are part of the Appalachian Range. The state has quiet towns, many with shaded greens and white, high-steepled churches. Connecticut also has many lakes. Winters are cold, but not too cold. Summers are hot, but not too hot. The state is poor in most natural resources, but stone, sand, and gravel are found there in abundance.

History

Several tribes of Algonkian-speaking Native Americans lived in Connecticut. One was the Mohegan, a branch of the Pequot tribe. *Quonecktacut* was the Algonkian name for the river. It meant "beside the long tidal river." Early settlers turned the word into "Connecticut" and called both the river and the land by this name.

A Dutch sea captain, Adriaen Block, discovered the Connecticut River in 1614. The Dutch set up a fort and trading post in Connecticut, but they never settled there permanently. English colonists, however, came from Massachusetts and founded the towns of Saybrook, Wethersfield, and New Haven. The English made the land their own. They defeated the Pequot Native Americans in a short, bloody war. They then drew up a plan of government believed to be the first formal

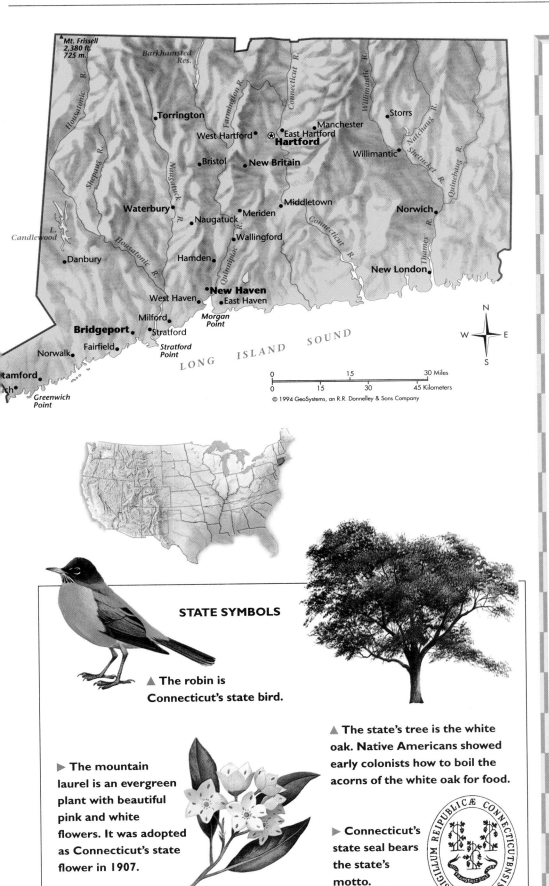

Mt. Frissell
2,380 ft.
725 m.

Barkhamsted Res.

Torrington

West Hartford • East Hartford
Manchester
⊛ Hartford

Storrs

Bristol • New Britain

Willimantic

Middletown

Norwich

Waterbury • Meriden

Naugatuck

Wallingford

Danbury

Hamden

New London

West Haven
New Haven
East Haven

Milford
Morgan Point

Bridgeport • Stratford
Stratford Point

Fairfield

Norwalk

LONG ISLAND SOUND

Greenwich Point

tamford

| 0 | | 15 | | 30 Miles |
| 0 | 15 | 30 | 45 Kilometers |

© 1994 GeoSystems, an R.R. Donnelley & Sons Company

N W E S

STATE SYMBOLS

▲ The robin is Connecticut's state bird.

▲ The state's tree is the white oak. Native Americans showed early colonists how to boil the acorns of the white oak for food.

► The mountain laurel is an evergreen plant with beautiful pink and white flowers. It was adopted as Connecticut's state flower in 1907.

► Connecticut's state seal bears the state's motto.

CONNECTICUT

Capital
Hartford (139,739 people)

Area
5,009 square miles (12,592 sq. km)
Rank: 48th

Population
3,287,116 people
Rank: 27th

Statehood
January 9, 1788 (Fifth of the 13 original states to ratify the Constitution)

Principal river
Connecticut

Highest point
Mount Frissell 2,380 feet (725 m)

Largest city
Bridgeport (141,686 people)

Motto
Qui Transtulit Sustinet ("He who transplanted still sustains")

Song
"Yankee Doodle"

Famous people
Ethan Allen, P. T. Barnum, Katharine Hepburn, Harriet Beecher Stowe, Noah Webster

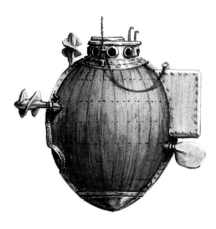

▲ David Bushnell's one-man submarine was built in Connecticut. The propeller had to be turned by hand.

▲ Connecticut resident Eli Whitney invented the cotton gin. The invention speeded up the production of cotton.

constitution ever written by a self-governing people. Connecticut was a British colony until 1776. In that year it became one of the 13 original states of the United States of America.

Also in 1776, David Bushnell of Connecticut built a one-man submarine. He named it the *American Turtle*. His craft was the first submarine ever used in the war. However, it was never successful in sinking British warships because it was not easily maneuvered.

Manufacturing in Connecticut

Up to the time of the Revolutionary War, nearly all manufacturing had been done by hand. But people now began to invent machines for manufacturing goods. England led the world in this work, but New England was not far behind.

Eli Whitney did much for the new manufacturing. This inventor was born in Massachusetts, but he lived and worked in Connecticut. His first invention was the cotton gin, a machine that removed the seeds from raw cotton. He built a factory for making cotton gins near New Haven, Connecticut.

Whitney set up a factory for making guns for the U.S. Army in 1798. Firearms had always been made slowly, one at a time. Only skilled gunsmiths, using hand tools, could make them. But Whitney invented machines that could manufacture all the parts of guns, and workers did not have to be highly skilled to use his machines. And his machines produced *interchangeable* parts for his guns, too. If a part broke, it could be easily, quickly, and cheaply replaced. Before Whitney's machines, a handmade part from one gun usually did not work in another gun of the same type.

Simeon North of Connecticut invented machines to make parts for pistols, and other Connecticut inventors did the same thing for making the parts of clocks. Soon even factory machinery could be made by machines, so factory machinery was produced faster and more cheaply. These advances made it easier to start factories, and manufacturing became the leading business in Connecticut.

Manufacturing helped spur the growth of cities throughout the state. Many persons left their farms and moved to cities to work in factories, where they could earn a better living. Factory jobs attracted many persons from other states and countries to settle in Connecticut. Today, the state has many small cities and more people for its size than almost any other state. Average annual incomes are higher than in any other state.

Insurance is also an important business in Connecticut. Hartford, the capital, is one of the world's biggest insurance centers, with the headquarters of many major insurance companies located there. It is also a center for banking.

Tourism is a thriving business in Connecticut. The Long Island Sound shoreline is a popular resort area. Tourists are also attracted to Mystic Seaport and Marinelife Aquarium, Yale University's Art Gallery and Peabody Museum, the Mark Twain and Harriet Beecher Stowe homes in Hartford, and the Foxwoods Casino in Ledyard, a famous gambling casino run by the Mashantucket Pequot Indians on their reservation. The state has many fine colonial buildings. Agriculture is still part of Connecticut's economy, too. Poultry, eggs, fruit, and shade-grown tobacco are the main items. The state's broadleaf tobacco is world-famous.

▶▶▶▶ **FIND OUT MORE** ◀◀◀◀
Statehood; Whitney, Eli

CONQUISTADOR

"This land is a whole new world," Amerigo Vespucci wrote of the Americas in the early 1500s. European explorers were soon challenged by the new territory. They believed that it would belong to the country whose flag flew over it. Spanish *conquistadors* (conquerors) claimed much of the land for Spain.

The conquistadors were explorers sent out by Spain to claim and govern territory in the New World. Many of these explorers heard sto-

▼ In 1533, Pizarro and his army invaded Peru and imprisoned the Inca king, Atahualpa. The king tried to buy his freedom by filling a room with gold. But Pizzaro executed him anyway.

ries of treasure and of cities built of gold. They hoped to make their fortunes by plundering these riches.

Spanish conquests of the Indians of the New World were bloody and violent. Their steel armor, gunpow-

der, and horses struck terror in the natives. In many cases, a few hundred Spanish soldiers overthrew ancient empires numbering tens of thousands of warriors. In Mexico, Hernando Cortés conquered the powerful Aztec kingdom of Montezuma. Francisco Pizarro, with fewer than 200 men, brutally gained control of the vast Inca empire of South America. The conquistadors were helped in their defeat of the Indians by the European diseases they brought with them. The Indians had no resistance to the new diseases and thousands died.

Some conquistadors failed to find wealth but made very important explorations. Vasco Núñez de Balboa crossed Panama and discovered the Pacific Ocean. Juan Ponce de León marched into Florida. Francisco Coronado and Hernando de Soto searched tirelessly for the fabled Seven Cities of Cibola. They found only Native American villages, but they were the first Europeans to explore what is now the southwestern United States. Jiminez de Quesada and Francisco Orellana combed the Andes and the Amazon for El Dorado, the Spanish name for an Indian king (and for his country). El Dorado was so rich, the stories said, that he took a bath in gold dust each year at a special festival. But the king was never found.

The ruthless and daring conquistadors destroyed entire civilizations in their quest for fame, gold and power. Millions of people died as a result of their actions, from wars and disease. They also carried the Spanish language, laws, religion, and way of life to two continents.

▶ ▶ ▶ ▶ **FIND OUT MORE** ◀ ◀ ◀ ◀
Aztecs; Balboa, Vasco Núñez De; Cibola, Seven Cities of; Coronado, Francisco; Cortés, Hernando; De Soto, Hernando; El Dorado; Inca; Pizarro, Francisco; Ponce De León, Juan; South America

▲ The conquistadors were soon followed by Roman Catholic missionaries. They used force if necessary to convert the Indians to Christianity. Here an Indian is being baptized.

▲ Francisco Pizzaro, conqueror of the Incas. He founded Lima (now the capital of Peru) before being murdered by a rival.

▲ Hernando Cortés, the conquistador who overthrew the Aztec empire and claimed it for Spain.

▲ **Joseph Conrad, the Polish-born author, is considered one of the great English story-tellers.**

▶ **The California condor is on the brink of extinction. Conservationists and the U.S. government are now trying to protect the species.**

CONRAD, JOSEPH (1857–1924)

Joseph Conrad is considered one of the greatest English novelists. His writings, marked by detailed descriptions, are about human weakness. He realized how difficult it is for people to lead a "good life."

He was born of Polish parents in what was then Russian Poland (now the Ukraine). His original name was Josef Teodor Konrad Nalecz Korzeniowski. At age 17, he left Poland to begin 20 years of seafaring life, serving first in the French and then in the British merchant marine. He learned English and worked his way from seaman to captain in the British Merchant Navy. The year he became captain, 1884, he also became a British citizen and changed his name to Joseph Conrad.

In 1894, Conrad retired from the sea, married, settled down in England, and began writing. His first novel, *Almayer's Folly,* was published in 1895.

Many of Conrad's tales were based on his experiences at sea, although the stories are about problems common to the human race. Conrad wrote about the many people he had met and the lands he had visited—Africa, the South Seas, and the East Indies.

Some of Conrad's best-known books are *An Outcast of the Islands, Lord Jim, Chance, Under Western Eyes, Victory, The Arrow of Gold,* and *The Rover.* Another famous tale, *Nostromo,* is set in South America and deals with the clash between making money and the fight for independence. Conrad wrote many brilliant short stories, too. *Heart of Darkness,* perhaps his greatest short story, is based on a voyage up the Congo River, in which the narrator learns about the evil in human nature.

▶▶▶ **FIND OUT MORE** ◀◀◀
Literature; Novel; Short Story

CONSERVATION

"We treat our Earth as though we had a spare," someone once said. Human beings have used soil, water, plants, animals, and minerals for nearly everything they make. Often we have wasted and destroyed these natural resources. *Conservation* means protecting resources and using them wisely. It also means preserving areas of natural beauty so that they can be used for recreation.

People did not bother much about conservation when North America was first settled. The continent was a land of great natural wealth. It had vast forests, numerous lakes and rivers, fertile soil, plentiful minerals such as coal and oil, and animals of all kinds.

The colonists thought that they would always have these resources because they were so plentiful. They were not careful about using them. When they wanted to clear land for farming, for example, they often burned down entire forests. This not only destroyed trees and killed many animals, but damaged the soil as well.

Trees and plants help to hold soil in place. When a forest is destroyed, rain can wash away the topsoil. This washing away, or *erosion,* spoils land for farming. The practice of one-crop farming in North America also harmed the soil.

Many farms in the South for instance, grew only tobacco, or only cotton. The plants used up certain minerals in the soil, and it quickly became worn out and useless. Nowadays people avoid this by using the system of *crop rotation*, whereby different crops are grown each year so that the soil is not depleted.

People have done great harm to our wildlife, too. Millions of bison once roamed the Great Plains. Before the white man came to North America, the Native Americans hunted bison. They killed the animals for food and clothing. White men shot them for sport, leaving the carcasses to rot on the prairie and to free the range for raising cattle. In the 1880s, only 550 bison were left.

Another example of what harm humans can do to wildlife is the story of the bald eagle. This courageous and powerful bird was chosen by Congress in 1782 as the official symbol of the United States. At the time, there were many bald eagles in North America. But hunters and farmers over the years killed nearly all of them because they endangered their livestock. The bald eagle is nearly extinct today. Pollution has also harmed these birds. Dumping sewage, garbage, and industrial wastes into our lakes and rivers has polluted the water. The pollution has poisoned the fish that live in the water. When the eagles feed on the fish, they are slowly poisoned, too.

▼ **Thousands of acres of trees have been destroyed to provide wood and paper. Eventually, we will run out of trees.**

Theodore Roosevelt, as President early in this century, began programs to save the country's natural resources. He set aside millions of acres of forest land. From this land, many national parks, including Yellowstone, were created. Gifford Pinchot became head of the newly created Forestry Service. The Bureau of Mines was established to find new mineral resources and better methods of mining. The U.S. Department of Agriculture began to teach farmers how to prevent erosion and how to restore worn-out soil through the use of fertilizers and efficient farming. During the Great Depression of the 1930s, the Civilian Conservation Corps (C.C.C.) was set up. It provided jobs in conservation for young men in national forests and parks across the country. Millions of seedlings planted by the C.C.C. have grown up into beautiful forests.

The conservation of our environment and its resources is now one of the greatest concerns internationally. All over the world governments have passed conservation laws. They have set up national parks and started programs to correct the damage that has already been done. There are also private organizations which work to "save the world." The Rio Summit, held in June 1992 in Rio de Janeiro, Brazil, was attended by several world leaders who discussed ways to conserve the environment.

Conservationists tackle many dif-

▲ **A boat owned by the international conservation group, Greenpeace.**

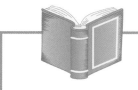

WHERE TO DISCOVER MORE

Ancona, George. *Riverkeeper.* New York: Macmillan, 1990.
Whitfield, Philip J. *Can the Whales Be Saved?* New York: Viking Kestrel, 1989.

Proportion of cities in 1990

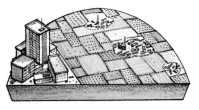

Proportion of cities in 2050?

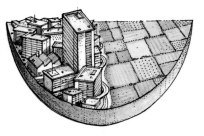

▲ **The growth of cities is threatening vast areas of our countryside. Cities may cover half of all land by 2050.**

▲ Oil spilled from ships kills millions of seabirds and fish every year. This guillemot is covered in oil. It cannot fly. If it tries to pick off the oil with its beak it swallows the sticky poison. It will die unless bird lovers clean it with detergent.

▼ John Constable's painting, *The Haywain,* created a sensation when first shown. See how he transformed a normal country scene into a beautiful picture.

ferent problems. For example, in Brazil they must stop the destruction of the rain forests. They have to deal with disasters such as the oil spills. In 1989, the *Exxon Valdez* supertanker spilled 11 million gallons of crude oil into the fertile waters off Alaska. During the Gulf War, Saddam Hussein deliberately poured millions of gallons of oil into the sea. In 1993, an oil tanker spewed oil onto the Shetland Islands, Scotland, killing thousands of animals.

Conservation is not only about big, international problems however. You can play a part too. For example, you can help by saving water when you shower, wash dishes, or brush your teeth. You can save electricity by turning off your lights, radios, and other appliances when they are not being used. By recycling bottles, cans, and newspapers, you help to conserve space in your town *landfill* (dump), save trees, and conserve energy. Never throw trash on the street. When you go on a picnic or camp out, always clean up before you leave. Be especially careful with matches and campfires because forest fires cause a great deal of damage.

▶▶▶▶ **FIND OUT MORE** ◀◀◀◀
Air Pollution; Ecology; Erosion; Flood; Forest Fire; Irrigation; Mines and Mining; National Forest; National Park; Pollution; Recycling; Roosevelt, Theodore; Soil; Water Pollution; Water Supply

CONSTABLE, JOHN
(1776–1837)

"I never saw an ugly thing in my life, for let the form of an object be what it will—light, shade, and perspective will make it beautiful." So said John Constable, the famous English artist. His painting, *The Haywain*, shown here, proves what he says. A hay wagon crossing a stream could be an ordinary scene. But he made it beautiful with the use of light in a glorious sky and by flashes of light and patches of shade in the water. He used shade beautifully in the trees, and his use of perspective and balance draws you into the scene.

Constable was born in East Bergholt, England. He was the second son of a miller. He painted from his own experience, but he depended on his rich imagination to make ordinary scenes interesting and beautiful. He knew farmers' carts, because he had played in them as a little boy. He had seen the barge horses on the Stour River wearing scarlet fringes on their collars, such as those that draw your eye into the picture.

Young John's parents expected him to join his father in the milling business, but John loved drawing and painting. At age 24, he went away to London to study at the Royal Academy schools. He had a long, slow start. He was so poor that he had to wait five years to get married. He kept on working, and the turning point in his career actually came with the painting shown here. The Haywain created a great sensation in 1824, when exhibited in France. Constable influenced French painters some years before the English realized he was a great artist. His ideas of changing light and shade were taken up 40 years after his death by the Impressionists.

CONSTANTINE

SEE ROMAN EMPIRE

CONSTELLATION

A *constellation* is a group of stars that makes a shape or picture. The stars seem to form patterns in the sky. For many people, the sky is a map of fairy tales and old legends. "Animals" hide among the stars. People and monsters from ancient myths "live" forever in the nighttime heavens.

Since earliest times, people have looked at the stars and found familiar patterns. One group of stars seems to look like a four-legged animal. Another group forms the shape of a royal throne. Look north and see if you can find the seven stars that some people call the Big Dipper, part of the constellation called the Great Bear. Orion is the mighty Hunter, placed in the sky by Artemis, goddess of hunting, who loved him. Pegasus is the Winged Horse of the hero Perseus, who also shines in the sky. The ancient Chinese thought that the constellation we call Pisces, the Fishes, was evil and caused great trouble on Earth.

Every constellation has its own legend. In ancient times, when people saw a group of stars in the shape of a horse, a bear, or a man, they wanted to know how such shapes got into the sky. So they made up stories to explain the shapes. Greek mythology tells about many constellations. The story of Orion actually tells how two constellations began.

The Greek god Zeus had twin children named Artemis and Apollo. Artemis was the goddess of hunting. She often traveled with Orion, a great hunter. This made Apollo jealous. One day Apollo tricked Artemis into shooting Orion. Her arrow killed him, and she was heartbroken. She changed Orion into stars. Another version is that Orion accidentally touched Artemis, and that she therefore summoned a huge scorpion to sting him to death. The constellation of the Scorpion is now on the far side of the sky from Orion.

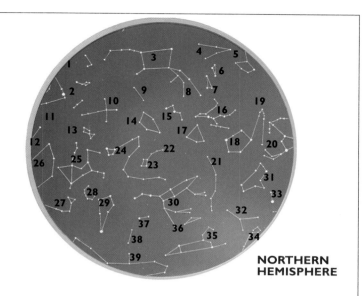

NORTHERN HEMISPHERE

Constellations of the Northern Hemisphere

1. Equuleus	11. Sagitta	21. Lynx	31. Gemini
2. Delphinus	12. Aquila	22. Pole (North) star	32. Cancer
3. Pegasus	13. Lyra	23. Ursa Minor	33. Canis Minor
4. Pisces	14. Cepheus	24. Draco	34. Hydra
5. Cetus	15. Cassiopeia	25. Hercules	35. Leo
6. Aries	16. Perseus	26. Ophiuchus	36. Leo Minor
7. Triangulum	17. Camelopardus	27. Serpens	37. Canes Venatici
8. Andromeda	18. Auriga	28. Corona Borealis	38. Coma Berenices
9. Lacerta	19. Taurus	29. Boötes	39. Virgo
10. Cygnus	20. Orion	30. Ursa Major	

Constellations of the Southern Hemisphere

1. Cetus	13. Sagittarius	25. Puppis	36. Centaurus
2. Sculptor	14. Aquila	26. Carina	37. Crux
3. Aquarius	15. Corona Australis	27. Volans	38. Musca
4. Piscis Austrinus	16. Pavo	28. Chamaeleon	39. Vela
5. Capricornus	17. Octans	29. Apus	40. Pyxis
6. Grus	18. Dorado	30. Triangulum Australe	41. Hydra
7. Phoenix	19. Pictor	31. Ara	42. Sextans
8. Fornax	20. Columba	32. Scorpio	43. Crater
9. Eridanus	21. Lepus	33. Serpens	44. Corvus
10. Hydrus	22. Orion	34. Ophiuchus	45. Libra
11. Tucana	23. Monoceros	35. Lupus	46. Virgo
12. Indus	24. Canis Major		

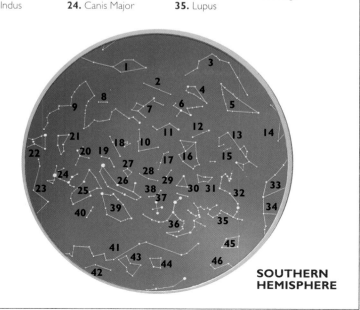

SOUTHERN HEMISPHERE

LEARN BY DOING

Next time you are out on a clear night, see if you can identify some of the constellations. The pictures with this article will help you. You will have to use your imagination to recognize some of the shapes. Find the Big Dipper. What direction are you facing when you see it? What direction do you face when you look at it two months later?

WHERE TO DISCOVER MORE

Berger, Melvin. *Star Gazing, Comet Tracking, and Sky Mapping.* New York: Putnam, 1985
Gustafson, John. *Stars, Clusters & Galaxies.* New York: Simon and Schuster, 1993.

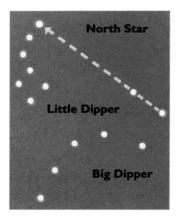

▲ The Big Dipper is part of a constellation called the Great Bear. Go out one clear night and look north. You should see the Big Dipper very easily. Its two brightest stars (the "Pointers") seem to point toward Polaris, the North Star. Polaris is at the end of the Little Dipper's handle.

Astronomers recognize 88 different constellations. Some can be seen only from the northern half of the world, others only from the southern half. The Little Dipper is such a constellation. The star at the end of the Little Dipper's handle is Polaris, the North Star. Polaris always seems to be almost exactly due north. Navigators in the Northern Hemisphere can use the North Star to find their way at night. The constellation Crux, the Southern Cross, is visible mainly from the Southern Hemisphere. (It can be seen just north of the equator, too.) It helps navigators to find their way in that part of the world.

Constellations have Latin names. Astronomers call the Little Dipper *Ursa Minor,* or "Little Bear." The Big Dipper is part of *Ursa Major,* or "Great Bear." Each star in a constellation also has a name, and Greek letters identify the stars according to brightness. The brightest star in the constellation *Pisces* ("the Fishes") is Alpha Piscium. The next brightest star is Beta Piscium, and so on. The brightest star in our skies is Alpha Canis Majoris, better known as Sirius. It is in the constellation *Canis Major* ("Great Dog").

Constellations appear and disappear from our skies as the Earth travels around the sun. During the winter, the Northern Hemisphere faces Orion at night. But six months later, on the opposite side of Earth's orbit around the sun, the part of Earth that faces Orion is in the daylight. As Earth moves around the sun, the constellations rise (come above the horizon) and set a few minutes earlier and slightly lower in the sky each day.

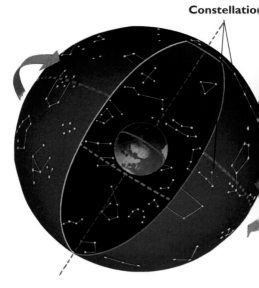

▲ A celestial sphere showing the constellations in relation to the Earth. The Earth is spinning on its axis so the constellations appear to move around the sky.

Some constellations (such as Orion) do not rise during nighttime for several months each year.

Twelve of the constellations follow paths near the section of sky traveled by the planets. This band across the sky is called the *zodiac.* The star shapes inside the band are the *constellations of the zodiac.* The planets appear to move through the constellations. The exact positions of the planets and the zodiac constellations are slightly different every minute. These changes in position are the basis of astrology.

The stars in constellations look close together because they are very far from Earth, but most of the stars are even farther from each other than they are from Earth. The constellations have changed shape slightly since they were named thousands of years ago. After millions of years the shapes will be gone altogether, and new constellations will fill the sky in their place.

▶▶▶▶ **FIND OUT MORE** ◀◀◀◀
Astrology; Astronomy; Mythology; Navigation; Star

CONSTITUTION, UNITED STATES

Have you ever heard people involved in an argument speak of their "constitutional rights"? Or condemn the Supreme Court for ruling a law "unconstitutional"?

The Constitution is the basic law of the United States. Among the men who wrote it were Alexander Hamilton, James Madison, and Thomas Jefferson, helped by Benjamin Franklin. They were influenced by the political theories of their age and by their own political experience as citizens of colonies ruled by Britain. They all worked for the independence of the colonies before and during the Revolutionary War. These great men believed that problems could be solved by reason. They had faith that society could be improved. They felt that progress should be expected.

The Constitution defines the Federal Government and describes the duties of its three main branches. The *Congress* has legislative power, with responsibility for making the laws of the country. The *President* has executive power to "preserve, protect, and defend the Constitution of the United States." The *Supreme Court* has judicial power, with authority to enforce the laws made by Congress. Each of these branches checks and balances the power of the other two.

The founding fathers did not want the government to have absolute power, as a king or queen does. So they limited the powers of the central government and left some powers to the states.

In its first ten amendments (also called the *Bill of Rights*) the Constitution establishes the basic freedoms of Americans, such as freedom of speech, of the press, of religion, and the freedom not to speak against oneself in court. The Bill of Rights is designed mainly to protect individual citizens against unlawful acts by their own government.

The Making of the Constitution

The Revolutionary War ended in 1781, and a peace treaty was signed with England in 1783. The 13 states, joined together loosely under the Articles of Confederation, soon began to squabble among themselves. Some states paid no attention to the laws and still openly opposed the rights of citizens. They disregarded jury trials, sentenced men to death without trials, closed down

The opening words of the United States Constitution are: "We, the people of the United States, in order to form a more perfect Union, establish justice, insure domestic tranquility, provide for the common defense, promote the general welfare, and secure the blessings of liberty to ourselves and our posterity, do ordain and establish this Constitution for the United States of America."

◄ Thomas Jefferson was one of the authors of the U.S. Constitution.

▼ The Constitution was discussed at a series of meetings held at Independence Hall, Philadelphia, in 1787. George Washington was president of the Constitutional Convention.

687

We the People of the United States, in order to form a more perfect Union, establish Justice, insure domestic Tranquility, provide for the common defence, promote the general Welfare, and secure the Blessings of Liberty to ourselves and our Posterity, do ordain and establish this Constitution for the United States of America.

Article I.

Section 1. All legislative Powers herein granted shall be vested in a Congress of the United States, which shall consist of a Senate and House of Representatives.

Section 2. The House of Representatives shall be composed of Members chosen every second Year by the People of the several States, and the Electors in each State shall have the Qualifications requisite for Electors of the most numerous Branch of the State Legislature.

▲ **The first few lines of the U.S. Constitution, one of the greatest documents ever written.**

▼ **The Constitution of the United States is on display at the National Archives in Washington, D.C.**

newspapers, and forcibly grabbed property. The leaders of the new country knew that a formal constitution must be written. But they probably did not know that they would create a document so effective and so timeless that it would function far into the 20th century and become a model for the governments of many other nations.

In May 1787, 55 delegates from 13 states gathered at Independence Hall in Philadelphia. They chose George Washington as president of the *Constitutional Convention*. The oldest of the delegates was 81-year-old Benjamin Franklin. James Madison took careful notes during the convention. His is the chief record we have of the delegates' debates and decisions.

The delegates to the Constitutional Convention soon divided into two groups. The "nationalists" wanted a strong central government with the power to declare war and make treaties, the power to trade with foreign nations, and the power to tax citizens. The "states'-righters" mistrusted strong national control and wished to make sure the rights of the states were respected. After a long summer of debate, the convention compromised. The "states'-righters" would have the protection they wanted in the establishment of a Senate composed of two representatives from each state, no matter how large or small in population. A larger legislative body, the House of Representatives, would also represent the people by states, but according to population. Together, these assemblies made up the United States Con-

gress. A Supreme Court also was established. The President would be elected by the people, rather than born to the job like a monarch, and Congress could remove the President from office if necessary.

The delegates signed the Constitution of the United States of America on September 17, 1787. Each individual state then approved, or *ratified*, the Constitution.

Changing the Constitution

On December 15, 1791, ten *amendments* (changes or additions) to the Constitution went into effect. These amendments, called the Bill of Rights, name and guarantee the rights of every citizen under the law. Other amendments were added as the United States grew. By 1986, there were 26 amendments.

Amendments may be made in two ways, according to the Constitution itself. A Constitutional Convention of delegates from every state may propose an amendment, but this method has been used only one time. A proposed amendment, called a *resolution*, may come from Congress. The resolution becomes law if two-thirds of the members of each house vote in favor of it, and if three-fourths of the state legislatures then ratify the amendment. The amendment may be ratified by special conventions in three-fourths of the states in place of legislative approval, but this has happened only once.

The Supreme Court is called the "guardian of the Constitution." Its duty is to interpret the laws and rights given in the Constitution or passed by Congress and signed by the

President. The Supreme Court can rule a state law "unconstitutional," thus canceling it. The Supreme Court can also declare an act of Congress illegal if the court does not think the act agrees with the meaning of the Constitution. This is known as the "power of judicial review."

▶▶▶▶ **FIND OUT MORE** ◀◀◀◀

Articles of Confederation; Bill of Rights; Congress, United States; Presidency; Revolutionary War; Supreme Court; United States Government

CONSTRUCTION

The construction of a building depends upon its function or purpose, its structure, and the materials from which it is built. Two important building functions are to protect people from the weather and to provide space for living and working. Some buildings such as theaters, schools, libraries, and churches, have special functions. Other buildings, such as the buildings in a zoo, have more than one function.

The structure of a building includes the parts of the building and the way they are put together. If a building is to be a large auditorium, its construction must allow for a broad, high room, to hold many people and to look spacious. Any kind of structure must be planned carefully, so that it does not fall down and carries out the building's function. If a building cannot support itself and the weight of all the people and things to be put into it, its structure is poor. If a museum is to show airplanes, then it must have a door wide enough to get the planes into the building and hallways wide enough for the planes to be moved from one room to another.

Building Materials

Materials are the basis of all buildings. There are three major kinds of materials. (1) Structural materials support the building, give it shape, form its protective "shell," and divide it into rooms. (2) Other materials protect the construction from weather or fire, or improve its appearance. (3) Different kinds of equipment supply heat, ventilation, light, and water.

The most important structural materials are wood, clay, stone, concrete, and steel. Each has special advantages and disadvantages. One or more of these materials is selected for a specific building depending on the advantages and disadvantages.

WOOD. Wood is an ancient building material, probably one of the first structural materials ever used. It is inexpensive, and it is easy to cut, shape, and fasten. Wood has three

WHERE TO DISCOVER MORE

Hauptly, Denis J. *A Convention of Delegates.* New York: Atheneum Publishers, 1987.

Maestro, Betsy. *A More Perfect Union.* New York: Lothrop, Lee & Shepard Books, 1987.

▼ **In Europe, the first farmers constructed the walls of their houses from woven twigs plastered with clay to protect them from the weather.**

▲ The Romans constructed stone aqueducts—structures for moving rivers over land. The arches were built around a light wooden framework. Each stone fit together exactly, so no mortar was needed.

features that make it useful in construction: It does not break easily when it is bent, as brick and stone do, and it is very strong— it can withstand a heavy load that presses down on it; and finally it is pliable—if a force bends the pieces of a wooden structure, the pieces "unbend" when the force is taken away. But wood must be protected by paint or other means. Unprotected wood can be eaten by insects, rotted by fungi, or ruined by wind and rain.

CLAY. Clay is used to make brick and tile. A wall of bricks, joined together by *mortar*, a kind of cement, can withstand very heavy weights. But such a wall is *brittle*. It cannot withstand forces that make it bend, unless it is very thick. Brick is cheap to make and easy to work with.

STONE. Stone is very strong and lasts a long time. It is an excellent building material, but it is expensive and difficult to handle. Stone must be cut from solid rock in a quarry. Many kinds of stone are shaped into blocks, trimmed to the desired size, and smoothed in order to fit tightly against other stones. Stone blocks are too heavy to move by hand, and a crane must be used to raise them into

place. A stone wall must also be thick, or a strong bending force will make it collapse.

STEEL. Steel is a wonderful building material. It lasts nearly as long as stone, is very strong, and, like wood, has some pliability. Steel can be formed into any shape. However, it must be painted or it will rust. Steel is used to form the superstructure, or skeleton, of modern skyscrapers.

CONCRETE. Concrete is a mixture of cement, sand, and gravel that dries into a rocklike mass. Many ancient peoples used concrete to "glue" stones together. The ancient Romans were probably the first people to do this. Modern engineers have found many uses for this substance. Along with steel, concrete is the most widely used structural material. Unlike stone, concrete does not have to be cut into blocks and fastened together. Wet concrete can be poured into wooden molds. When the concrete dries, it forms a solid structure the shape of the mold.

Concrete by itself withstands very great forces that push down on it. Like stone or brick, concrete is brittle. But *reinforced* concrete—concrete that has steel rods in it—takes on the pliability of steel. Reinforced concrete can withstand bending and stretching forces. However, concrete quickly becomes stained and can look unattractive.

OTHER MATERIALS. Few buildings contain only structural parts. Most buildings have glass windows to let in light and let the people inside look out (or let the people outside look in). Buildings are usually insulated, to help keep the inside cool in summer and warm in winter. And most buildings have complicated heating, cooling, lighting, plumbing, and electrical systems. These systems use up miles of metal, plastic, and wood. Paint and wallpaper are also used in almost every type of building to decorate and protect the internal structural materials.

Building a Skyscraper

Constructing a skyscraper or any other large building takes a long time. Many people with many different kinds of training take part. An architect and several different kinds of engineers design the building and the heating, plumbing, and other systems that any building includes. When all the plans and the hundreds of drawings are complete, the builder goes to work.

If a tall building were built on soft soil, the building would sink. So the building company's first job is to *excavate* (dig) a hole for the basements and to lay the foundation—the building's support. Bulldozers, steam shovels, and trucks appear at the building site. Following carefully planned marks, they dig a deep hole. Some skyscrapers have five or even more basements!

When the bottom of the hole is smoothed out, special machines lay the foundation. This can be done in two ways. A pile driver, a kind of giant motorized hammer, can pound long steel poles, called *piles*, down through the soft soil to the bedrock beneath it. A newer, stronger method is to use a special digging machine that digs narrow holes down through the soil to the rock. Workers then pour concrete into the holes. The concrete hardens into very strong supports that are called *caissons*.

When the foundation is complete, workers begin to erect the frame, the steel skeleton that supports the weight of the building. Cranes move each piece of steel into place, and workers fasten the pieces together. Riveting and welding were once used to join steel pieces, but bolts are quicker and easier to work with.

Some buildings have concrete frames. To erect such a frame, workers build wooden forms, put steel rods into them, and fill them with concrete. When the concrete sets, or hardens, the workers remove the wooden forms, and the concrete frame is ready.

The next step is to construct the floors and the roof. Workers build a temporary wooden floor, then pour reinforced concrete onto it. When the concrete sets, the wooden floor is removed. Other workers then begin to put up the outside walls. The frame holds the weight of the building. The walls simply form a kind of shell that surrounds the building. Many skyscrapers have walls made mostly of glass. Sometimes thin stone, metal, or plastic slabs are used. The wall is hung on the frame in sections, much as curtains are hung on a window frame. The walls of frame buildings are called *curtain walls*.

The shell of the building is complete when the walls are up. But much work must still be done. Workers install partitions that divide each floor into rooms. If it is part of the plan, these walls will be plastered. Still other workers put in the complicated systems that carry heat, water, and electric power all through the building. The elevators must be installed. The ceilings will probably be soundproofed and the floors covered with tile. Decorators and painters take over, and when they are through, the building is ready for use.

▲ The world's first skyscraper was the Home Insurance Building in Chicago. It was built in 1885 and was only ten stories high. Its brick walls were self-supporting, but its floors were supported by an iron and steel frame.

A building permit gives a person the legal right to build a structure. It also gives community officials the right to inspect the structure to make sure that the builder has not violated the building code (regulations).

◄ The Sears Tower in Chicago is the tallest building in the world. It has 110 stories. The Eiffel tower in Paris, France, was constructed of more than 7,000 tons of iron.

▼ **This 80-story tower,** *La Tour Sans Fin* **(the tower without end), is due to be constructed in Paris, France, in the 1990s.**

Building a House

Houses today are usually built in much the same way as they were hundreds of years ago, before construction machines were invented. A house does not need to stand on piles because it is not that heavy. And its frame does not have to be steel or concrete. It can be wood, which is much easier to work with. In fact, houses or other small buildings need not have frames at all. Special walls, called *bearing walls*, may replace the frame and support the weight of the building. A building may have bearing walls if its walls are brick, stone, or concrete. The lightness of the floors and roofs they support make them practical for houses. Before steel framing, some tall buildings had bearing walls that were more than 6 feet (1.8 m) thick.

One reason that houses cost so much money is that they are often built using slow, old-fashioned methods. Two new construction methods have come into use. *Prefabricated* and *modular* construction can provide good houses at lower cost. "Prefabricated" means "made ahead of time." The walls and roof of a prefabricated house are built in sections in a factory. Doors, windows, and electrical wiring are built into the sections. All the parts are loaded on a truck and driven to the place where the house is wanted. Workers connect the sections to a basement that is built before the sections arrive, attach the sections to one another, connect the house to gas, water, and electrical lines, and put on the roof. People may move into their new house in only a few days.

Modular construction is also very quick and easy. Modules are sections that can easily be connected to one another. One module might be a living room, another might be a dining room and kitchen, and other modules might be bedrooms, recreation rooms, and garages. Modules are built in a factory, then hooked together where the house will stand. The people who buy a modular house can choose how many rooms they want and the arrangement of the rooms. A prefabricated house must be built exactly as it was designed. Both of these construction techniques will become more and more important because they offer good houses quickly at a low price.

▶▶▶▶**FIND OUT MORE** ◀◀◀◀
Architecture; Building Material; Caisson; Carpentry; Concrete; Empire State Building; House; Quarrying; Streets and Roads; Wood

☼ CONTACT LENSES

For many years eyeglasses were the only way to correct problems with *vision*, or the way that people see. But some people find them uncomfortable. Athletes risk injury if eyeglass *lenses* break. And other people simply dislike how they look with eyeglasses.

Contact lenses solve these problems while doing the same job as eyeglasses. They are eyeglasses that are worn directly on the surface of the eyes. It is almost impossible to tell whether someone is wearing contact lenses.

There are two types of contact lenses, *hard* and *soft*. Hard lenses are made of clear plastic or silicon. They cover the *iris*, or colored part of the eyeball, and float on a thin layer of tears. Soft plastic lenses become soft and pliable when wet. They are more comfortable than hard lenses, but require more care. Hands should be clean when inserting contact lenses, or an infection might occur.

Contact lenses are more effective than eyeglasses. By letting people see clearly whichever way they look, rather than just straight ahead, they provide a wider *field of vision*.

▶▶▶▶**FIND OUT MORE** ◀◀◀◀
Eye; Glasses; Lens; Sight

CONTINENT

The largest land areas of the Earth are called continents. They are nearly or completely surrounded by oceans. The continents take up less than one-quarter of the Earth's surface, but they total nine-tenths of the land area. (About seven-tenths of the Earth's surface is covered by water.) There are seven continents—Africa, Antarctica, Asia, Australia, Europe, North America, and South America. The Arctic region is not a continent because it is made up mostly of water, much of which is frozen, forming vast snow-covered icebergs.

Continents are vast masses of light rock floating on the heavier rock that makes up most of the Earth's crust. A continent is much longer and wider than it is deep. It is usually higher inland than near the edges. The highest points of the continent are called *continental divides*.

Scientists now believe that all the continents were one huge continent about 170 million years ago. This "supercontinent," called *Pangaea*, slowly broke up, and its pieces drifted apart and are still moving. Before Pangaea formed, about 280 million years ago, there were several continents, like today, but those continents were very different from the ones that we now know.

Scientists believe that the North and South Poles were once in very different places in relation to the continents. Fossil discoveries show that Western Europe once supported tropical life, and forests used to grew in what is now Antarctica.

Continental Shelves

In most places, the edges of the continents slope gently downward into the oceans before making a sharper drop to the deep ocean floor. The part of a continent under the ocean is called a *continental shelf*. The usual width of a continental shelf is about 40 miles (64 km), but there are many

Continent	Area	Highest Point	Lowest Point
Africa	11,703,915 square miles (30,313,000 sq. km)	Kilimanjaro, Tanzania, 19,340 feet (5,895 m)	Qattara Depression, Egypt, 440 feet (134 m) below sea level
Antarctica	5,400,000 square miles (14,000,000 sq. km)	Vinson Massif, 16,860 feet (5,139 m)	Sea level
Asia	17,135,370 square miles (44,380,400 sq. km)	Mount Everest, Nepal-Tibet, 29,028 feet (8,848 m)	Dead Sea, Israel-Jordan, 1,296 feet (395 m) below sea level
Australia	2,967,909 square miles (7,686,848 sq. km)	Mount Kosciusko New South Wales, 7,316 feet (2,230 m)	Lake Eyre, south Australia, 36 feet (11m) below sea level
Europe	4,006,743 square miles (10,534,600 sq. km)	Mount Elbrus, Russia 18,481 feet (5,633 m)	Caspian Sea, Eastern Europe 92 feet (27 m) below sea level
North America	9,072,243 square miles (23,497,000 sq. km)	Mount McKinley, Alaska, 20,320 feet (6,193 m)	Death Valley, California, 280 feet (85 m) below sea level
South America	6,879,183 square miles (17,817,000 sq. km)	Aconcagua, Argentina, 22,831 feet (6,959 m)	Salina Grande, Argentina, 131 feet (40 m) below sea level

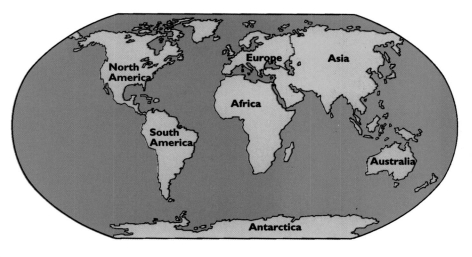

exceptions. The shelf is completely missing along the western coast of South America. And off the Arctic coasts of Europe and Russia, the shelf extends for 750 to 800 miles (1,200–1,300 km), making the Arctic Ocean very shallow. Some continental shelves have higher parts that appear above the water as islands.

The edges of continental shelves are an average of 430 feet (130 m) beneath the surface of the ocean. Some may be as deep as 600 feet

▲ The major land masses on the surface of the Earth are known as the continents.

▼ **A painting showing the members of the First Continental Congress. The group wanted rights for the colonies but not independence from Britain.**

(180 m). The edge of the shelf drops very sharply, forming a *continental slope* that leads to the bottom of the ocean floor.

▶ ▶ ▶ ▶ **FIND OUT MORE** ◀ ◀ ◀ ◀
Continental Divide; Continental Drift; Geology; Island; Plate Tectonics

CONTINENTAL CONGRESS

The Continental Congress was an organization representing the original 13 colonies. The First Continental Congress met in Philadelphia from September through October, 1774. Delegates from all the 13 colonies except Georgia drew up the *Declaration of Rights*. They listed what they believed their rights as English colonists should be. They wanted representative government, the right to assemble, and trials before juries. Delegates to the Congress agreed that the colonies should not buy any goods from Britain or sell any goods to Britain until their complaints were satisfactorily settled.

Fighting between colonists and British soldiers soon broke out in Massachusetts. The Second Continental Congress met in Philadelphia from May 1775 to early December 1776. Delegates from Georgia

attended for the first time. The delegates organized a Continental Army to oppose the British and appointed George Washington, a delegate, as commander-in-chief. They also issued a declaration stating their reasons for taking up arms and made a final, but futile, attempt to persuade Britain to recognize their rights. Representatives were sent to foreign countries, notably to France, to obtain help for the colonists' cause.

After the outbreak of war, the Second Continental Congress urged the colonies to establish their own local governments, independent of Britain. Money was issued to carry on the war. On June 7, 1776, Richard Henry Lee of Virginia proposed that the 13 colonies be "free and independent states." Thomas Jefferson, John Adams, Alexander Hamilton, and others, helped by Benjamin Franklin, were asked to write a formal Declaration of Independence, which was approved by the Congress on July 4, 1776 at Independence Hall in Philadelphia. (The Fourth of July is today known as Independence Day in the United States and is a national holiday.)

The Third Continental Congress met from late December 1776 to March 1781. It had to move from one city to another several times, to avoid the fighting. It took over direction of the war. The Congress agreed in 1777 on a plan to unite the 13 states into one nation. The plan was outlined in the Articles of Confederation, the nation's first constitution. This constitution was sent to the states and agreed to by 1781. By this plan, a new Congress of the Confederation replaced the Continental Congress. A more complete and stronger plan, the U.S. Constitution, was adopted in 1789.

▶ ▶ ▶ ▶ **FIND OUT MORE** ◀ ◀ ◀ ◀
Articles of Confederation; Constitution, United States; Declaration of Independence; Revolutionary War

CONTINENTAL DIVIDE

If you had been a boy or girl in a wagon train heading west in pioneer days, at the Continental Divide your wagon would have been 7,550 feet (2,300 m) above sea level. You would have been following the Oregon Trail over the Rocky Mountains, through South Pass. That might have meant high winds and snow, and possibly death.

The Divide is the imaginary line that runs north to south through North America, along the highest peaks of the Rocky Mountains. Rain falling west of it drains through rivers that flow toward the Pacific Ocean; rivers east of the Divide flow toward the Mississippi. The Divide is therefore called the continent's *watershed*.

The Divide of North America runs from Canada through Montana, Wyoming, Colorado, and New Mexico, then through Mexico. A lower divide runs across North America from east to west, separating those rivers that flow north to the Gulf of St. Lawrence, Hudson Bay, and the Arctic Ocean from those that flow south to the Mississippi and the Gulf of Mexico.

CONTINENTAL DRIFT

If you look at a map of the world you will notice immediately that Africa seems as if it might fit snugly against South America. Over the centuries many people have suggested that the two continents were once joined together, but it was not until 1912 that someone put forward a serious display of evidence that continents do indeed "drift" around the surface of our planet. That man's name was Alfred Wegener.

Today continental drift is regarded as an established fact. The modern version of the theory is called *plate tectonics* because it is believed that the *surface* (crust) of the earth is made up of a number of rigid plates that float on the molten rock of the mantle beneath. It is these plates, rather than merely the continents that ride upon some of them, which "drift" relative to each other.

▶ ▶ ▶ ▶ **FIND OUT MORE** ◀ ◀ ◀ ◀
Continent; Earth; Plate Tectonics

CONVECTION

HEAT AND COLD

CONVENT

SEE MONASTERY

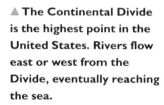

▲ The Continental Divide is the highest point in the United States. Rivers flow east or west from the Divide, eventually reaching the sea.

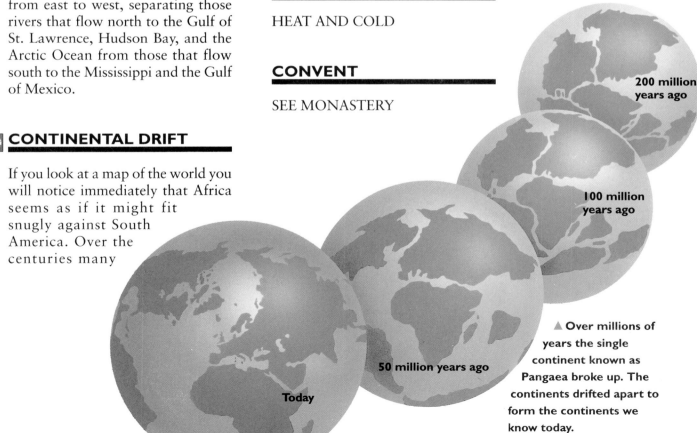

▲ Over millions of years the single continent known as Pangaea broke up. The continents drifted apart to form the continents we know today.

200 million years ago

100 million years ago

50 million years ago

Today

▲ **Captain James Cook, English navigator and explorer.**

▼ **This family gathers around the table for a holiday feast.**

COOK, CAPTAIN JAMES (1728–1779)

James Cook, an English navigator and explorer, discovered Australia and the Hawaiian Islands on three famous voyages to the South Pacific. Cook was born in Yorkshire, England. He joined the British Navy and became an expert surveyor and astronomer. He helped map the St. Lawrence River and the coasts of Labrador and Newfoundland.

Cook set out in 1768 in the ship *Endeavour* on his first historic voyage to the Pacific, hoping to find "Terra Australis," a great continent believed to exist in the far south. On this voyage he visited Tahiti and New Zealand, and explored the east coast of Australia, claiming it for Britain.

In 1772, Captain Cook sailed again from England with two ships, *Resolution* and *Adventure*, on his longest voyage. He traveled about 70,000 miles (113,000 km) in three years, sailing across the Antarctic Circle for the first time in recorded history, and discovering New Caledonia and the Cook Islands.

He set sail on his third expedition in 1776, in the ships *Resolution* and *Discovery*, looking for the Northwest Passage—a way to sail from the northern Atlantic Ocean to the northern Pacific Ocean. (It was not to be discovered until 1903–1906 by the Norwegian explorer, Roald Amundsen.) On this voyage Cook discovered the Hawaiian Islands in 1778. He sailed along and surveyed the west coast of North America from Oregon to the Arctic Ocean, through the Bering Strait. Cook then returned to the Hawaiian Islands, where he was killed in a fight with some islanders over a boat stolen from one of his vessels.

▶▶▶▶ **FIND OUT MORE** ◀◀◀◀
Australia; Exploration; Hawaii

COOKING

No one knows how human beings discovered cooking. A famous English writer, Charles Lamb, once wrote a funny essay, "A Dissertation on Roast Pig." Lamb wrote about a Chinese man whose house burned down while his pig was inside it. The man happened to taste the cooked meat of the pig and discovered it tasted better than the raw meat he had always eaten. So to get more of the tasty cooked meat the man and his neighbors kept burning down houses with pigs inside. How do you think people *really* discovered cooking? However it was discovered, cooking makes most foods taste better. It also kills harmful bacteria.

Learn to Cook

Learning to cook is fun. It is easy to cook when you learn the correct and safe way to do it. There are certain basic ways to prepare and cook food. The basic cooking methods include baking, frying, roasting, boiling, broiling, stewing, poaching, and barbecuing. These methods are explained in the table. There are many kinds of utensils—pots and

pans, measuring cups and spoons, forks and knives, and bowls—that you use in cooking.

Understanding how your family's stove works is also very important. Is it a gas stove or electric? How do you turn the heat off and on? Stoves can be dangerous so ask an adult to show you how to operate a stove safely.

A *recipe* lists the *ingredients*—what kinds of foods are needed—and gives the amount of each ingredient needed for a particular dish. A recipe also tells you, step by step, how to prepare the dish you've decided to cook.

Below is a recipe for hamburgers. Perhaps you would like to try it. First check to see if you have the necessary ingredients and utensils in your kitchen. When you have everything, measure the ingredients carefully to get the exact amount the recipe calls for. You'll need to use special marked measuring spoons and cups that are exactly the right size.

Simple Hamburgers
1 pound (450 g) ground beef or chuck
¾ teaspoon salt
¼ cup milk
1 tablespoon ice water

Lightly mix together in a bowl the meat, salt, milk, and water. With your hands, shape the meat mixture into four round patties about one inch (2.5 cm) thick. Be careful not to press the meat together too solidly, or the patty will be too heavy. Put the patties in a broiling pan. Broil them until they are browned on one side. Then use a spatula to turn them to brown on the other side. Cook both sides for three to five minutes, or until the hamburgers are done the way you like. If you cook them too long, however, they will taste very dry. Put the finished hamburgers on top of a paper towel on a plate so that the towel will absorb any excess grease. Remove the towel and serve the hamburgers either by themselves or inside hamburger buns.

Can you think of other ways to make hamburgers? You might like to add spices or herbs to give your hamburgers a special flavor. Try a teaspoon of thyme, ginger, curry, garlic or chili powder. But not all at once! Maybe you'd rather add breadcrumbs or crushed cornflakes. How about some tomato catsup or mild mustard? Experiment by making tiny hamburgers. On each hamburger sprinkle a bit of a different spice or herb, or add whatever you like.

After you cook the hamburgers, sample each one to see which kinds you like best. This would be fun to do with your friends, too. Half the fun of cooking is creating your own special dishes and being daring enough to cook something quite different from what you usually eat.

If you cook a whole meal, of course, you'll want to serve more than hamburgers. You'll want to have a well-balanced meal with meat or fish, a green or yellow vegetable, a starchy vegetable, fruit, milk, and dessert. Here is a recipe for potato salad, which you might want to serve with your hamburgers.

Potato Salad
4 medium-sized potatoes, washed
3 eggs
1 cup chopped celery
¼ cup chopped onion
¼ cup pickle relish
¼ teaspoon pepper
¼ cup mustard
½ cup mayonnaise
salt
paprika

Cut each potato in half, put them in a pot and cover them with water. Add one teaspoon of salt. Cover the pot and boil the potatoes over medium heat for 20 to 25 minutes, or until the potato skins start to peel off. The potatoes are cooked when you can easily push a fork into them. Drain off the hot water, but be careful that you don't get burned. Cover the potatoes with cold water to cool them.

▲ **A restaurant chef prepares a delicious meal.**

COMMON TERMS USED IN COOKING

Baking means in the oven with little or no liquid.

Barbecuing means on a grill over an open flame, usually outdoors on charcoal.

Boiling means in bubbling hot liquid, at boiling point.

Broiling means under the oven's broiler.

Frying means on top of the stove in hot fat or oil.

Microwaving means in a microwave oven.

Poaching means in simmering liquid that covers the food.

Roasting means in the oven with little or no liquid.

Simmering means in liquid, but under boiling point.

Steaming means with steam from a boiling liquid.

Stewing means in liquid, below boiling point, usually for a long time.

CALVIN COOLIDGE
THIRTIETH
PRESIDENT

AUGUST 3, 1923–
MARCH 4, 1929

Born: July 4, 1872, Plymouth, Vermont

Parents: John Calvin and Victoria Josephine Moor Coolidge

Education: Amherst College

Religion: Congregational

Occupation: Lawyer

Political party: Republican

State represented: Massachusetts

Married: 1905 to Grace Anna Goodhue (1879–1957)

Children: two sons (one of whom died at birth)

Died: January 5, 1933, Northampton, Massachusetts

Buried: Plymouth, Vermont

Meanwhile, cover the eggs with water in a saucepan and heat the water until it boils. Turn off the heat and let the eggs stand (covered) for 20 minutes. Remove them from the hot water with a slotted spoon, and put them in cold water.

Place the cooled potatoes on a wooden cutting board and carefully pull off the skins. Hold each potato with a fork while you peel it with a small knife. Ask an adult to show you how to cut the potatoes into small cubes. Put these into a large bowl.

Next, ask an adult to help you carefully chop up the celery and onion on a cutting board. Now the eggs should be cool enough for you to peel and slice. Sprinkle the potatoes with ¼ teaspoon of salt. Add the eggs, celery, onion, pickle relish, mustard, pepper, and paprika to the potatoes. Toss all the ingredients together gently and cover the bowl. Chill it in the refrigerator for at least four to six hours. Add the mayonnaise just before you serve the salad.

Gingerbread Faces
1 box of gingerbread mix
⅓ cup raisins
maraschino cherries cut in half
(if you wish)

Make the gingerbread according to the instructions on the box. As soon as you remove the cake pan from the oven, gently make lines with a knife on the top of it to mark off the gingerbread squares.

Use the raisins to make a different face on each square. Make the eyes horizontal, vertical, or slanted. Give some faces large noses by using a big raisin. Give another one a pointed nose by poking the narrow end of the raisin into the cake. See how many different-shaped mouths you can create. If you have the cherries, use them to make bright mouths and noses. Gingerbread is good to eat either warm or cold.

When you have learned how to make hamburgers, potato salad, and gingerbread faces, you will be able to cook a whole meal.

▶▶▶▶ **FIND OUT MORE** ◀◀◀◀
Baking and Bakeries; Food; Nutrition; Vegetarian

COOLIDGE, CALVIN (1872–1933)

President Warren G. Harding died in a San Francisco hotel on August 2, 1923. In the very early morning of August 3, Vice President Calvin Coolidge was notified that he was now President. Coolidge was visiting his father's farm near Plymouth, Vermont. His father, a justice of the peace, administered the oath of office. Coolidge was re-elected

▶ **President Calvin Coolidge opened the 1925 World Series.**

President in the 1924 election.

As a boy, John Calvin Coolidge helped with the work on the farm in Vermont. He was graduated from Amherst College in Massachusetts. After serving in several lesser public offices, he became governor of Massachusetts in 1919. The Boston police went on strike while Coolidge was governor. With no police to stop them, criminals broke into stores and robbed people. Governor Coolidge called in the state militia to act as policemen. He said, "There is no right to strike against the public safety by anybody, anywhere, anytime."

Leaders in the Republican Party liked the firm way that the governor handled the strike. They nominated Coolidge for Vice President at the Republican Convention in 1920. Harding and Coolidge won the presidential election.

Coolidge was a well-liked President, although he had a widespread reputation for saying very little. He was an upright New England Yankee. He believed in hard work and thrift. He even used to keep track of White House expenses. As President, he reduced the national debt by several billion dollars. He also lowered everyone's income taxes by seeing that the government spent less money. Coolidge was President during a time of great prosperity. He refused to sign many laws that would have given the government more control over business. He said, "When things are going all right, it is a good plan to let them alone."

The prosperity while Coolidge was President was followed by the Great Depression during President Hoover's term. The former President was saddened and bewildered by this disaster. He spent his last years in Northampton, Massachusetts, where he had once been mayor.

▶▶▶▶ **FIND OUT MORE** ◀◀◀◀
Depression; Economics;
Harding, Warren G.; Presidency

COOPER, JAMES FENIMORE (1789–1851)

The first important author to use North American scenes and characters in his books was James Fenimore Cooper. His descriptions of North America's forests and prairies are not only beautiful but historically important. They are early descriptions of places where the pioneers lived. Cooper also showed the clash between the frontier and advancing civilization.

Cooper was born in New Jersey. When he was one year old, his father moved the family to Otsego Lake in New York, where he founded Cooperstown. The area was a wilderness, and many Native Americans lived nearby. Cooper later went to Yale University but was expelled. He then joined the U.S. Navy. Three years later, Cooper left the Navy and was married.

Cooper wrote his first book, *Precaution*, after his wife dared him to write a better book than the English one he was reading. *Precaution* was a failure, but his next book, *The Spy*, a story of the Revolutionary War, was a success. Cooper's most famous works, the *Leatherstocking Tales*—written between 1823 and 1841—are The *Pioneers*, *The Last of the Mohicans*, *The Prairie*, *The Pathfinder*, and *The Deerslayer*. The books are about pioneers and Native Americans in the American wilderness. Cooper wrote a total of 50 books, including several sea adventures.

▶▶▶▶ **FIND OUT MORE** ◀◀◀◀
Literature; Novel; Pioneer Life

▲ James Fenimore Cooper, great U.S. writer of early frontier adventures.

President Coolidge was nicknamed "Silent Cal" because he spoke very little. A woman once told him she had made a bet that she could get him to say more than two words. "You lose," replied the President.

▲ A scene from Fenimore Cooper's *The Last of the Mohicans*, a tale set during the French and Indian War.

▲ Copernicus, who promoted the idea that Earth and the other planets go around the sun.

▶ Copernicus' idea of our solar system. He thought the planets went around the sun in circles. Only later did Kepler show that the orbits were ellipses.

▼ U.S. composer Aaron Copland conducting a recording of one of his own works.

COPERNICUS, NICOLAUS (1473–1543)

In the early 1500s, almost everyone believed that the sun, the planets, and all the other heavenly bodies revolved around (circled) the Earth. No one had questioned that "fact" for more than 1,000 years. But a Polish cleric and astronomer, Niklas Koppernigk, who took the Latin name Nicolaus Copernicus, had a different view of things. Copernicus's new ideas caused a revolution in the thinking of astronomers.

Copernicus was trained not only in mathematics but also in medicine and church law. He spent most of his life serving as both a church official and a doctor in the town of Frauenburg, Poland. He also spent much time studying astronomy. He made observations of the positions of the sun, moon, planets, and stars. Copernicus was convinced from his studies that the Earth and the other planets really revolve around the sun. He realized that the sun and stars seem to be revolving around the Earth because the Earth itself is turning on its axis.

Copernicus wrote a book about his ideas. Because the ideas were so new, and because he was frightened of persecution, it took a long time to get the book published—13 years after he wrote it. He saw the first printed copy when he was on his deathbed.

▶▶▶▶ **FIND OUT MORE** ◀◀◀◀
Astronomy; Solar System

COPLAND, AARON (1900–1990)

Aaron Copland helped develop a music that was clearly American. He did this both in his own composing and by helping young composers.

Copland was born in Brooklyn, New York, and began piano lessons early. He was studying harmony and trying to write music even before he graduated from high school. He decided not to go to college, so that he would have more time for music. He studied musical composition in Paris, France, and began his musical career there.

His first large work, *Symphony for Organ and Orchestra*, was first performed in 1925 by the New York Symphony Orchestra. From that time, Copland composed, taught, and helped promote U.S. music. His early compositions used jazz material. His ballet *Billy the Kid* contained cowboy songs, and Mexican folk music sparked the orchestral piece *El Salón Mexico*. Copland wrote symphonies, operas, music for piano, scores for movies, and books on music.

The poet Carl Sandburg spoke Abraham Lincoln's words at the first performance of Copland's *Lincoln Portrait*, a work for orchestra and narrator. *Appalachian Spring*, music written for dancer Martha Graham, won a Pulitzer Prize. In 1949, he won an Academy Award for the music for the motion picture, *The Heiress*.

▶▶▶▶ **FIND OUT MORE** ◀◀◀◀
Composer; Dance; Music

COPPER

Copper is a soft metallic element that has many uses. It has been an important part of human life for more than 5,000 years. Copper is used in cooking utensils, coins, pipes, and electrical wires.

Pure copper is a reddish-brown metal. This copper is too soft to be used for the same purposes as iron or steel. Instead, copper is mixed with other metals to produce strong *alloys*, such as bronze and brass. The ability to make bronze helped humans emerge from the Stone Age.

Copper has four important qualities. It is a good *conductor* (transmitter) of heat and electricity. That is why copper is used for pots and pans, as well as for electrical wiring. Only silver, which is expensive, conducts electricity better than copper.

Copper is also *malleable*, or easy to shape into forms. This quality is useful in making curved pipes for plumbing. Copper items also resist

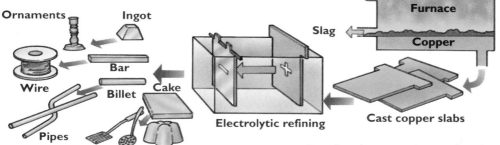

corrosion, so they do not rust.

The fourth quality of copper is its *ductility*, which means that it can be drawn out or stretched without breaking. This makes copper ideal as a material for electrical wires.

▶▶▶▶ FIND OUT MORE ◀◀◀◀
Alloy; Electricity; Element; Heat and Cold; Metal

COPYRIGHT

SEE PATENTS AND COPYRIGHTS

CORAL

If you are lucky, you may have found some coral on a beach. Maybe it looked and felt like white stone with an interesting shape or design. Possibly it was a lacy sea fan or a many-branched sea whip tinted green or lavender.

◀How copper is separated from copper ore. The ore is crushed into small pieces, and then ground into fine particles to form a slurry. The slurry is heated in a furnace to separate the copper. A converter purifies the molten copper using electrolytic refining. The final processing stage consists of melting and casting the copper into cakes, billets, bars, and ingots.

Coral *polyps* are tiny, soft animals that live in the ocean. They are called *anthozoans* or "flower-animals." They are simple living "cylinders" that spend their lives anchored in one place. They eat tiny particles of sea life, which they trap with their tentacles. Corals are *coelenterates* and are related to jellyfish.

Many kinds of coral polyps remove calcium from ocean water and pro-

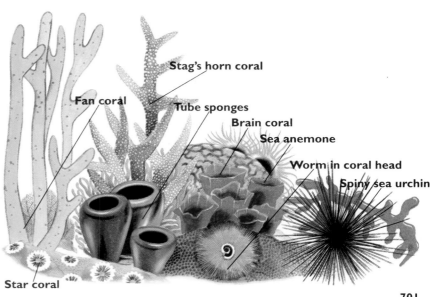

▼Some of the many different types of coral and the creatures that live in the coral rock. Coral is made up of the hard shells of millions of dead sea creatures, called coral polyps.

duce a hard material called *corallite*, or *calcium carbonate* (limestone). This material forms a cup around the soft polyp. When the polyp dies, the corallite remains behind, like a skeleton. We call this skeleton "coral". The coral can be brightly-colored.

Not all coral animals form corallite. The *stinging coral* of tropical waters makes a spongy coating on rocks. Its polyps have stinging cells that can give painful rashes to swimmers.

▶▶▶▶ **FIND OUT MORE** ◀◀◀◀
Coelenterate; Great Barrier Reef; Island

▼ **Australia's Great Barrier Reef, formed of coral, is the largest structure ever made by living creatures.**

CORAL SEA

The Coral Sea lies off the northeastern coast of Australia in the southern Pacific Ocean. It touches New Guinea to the north and Vanuatu and the Solomon Islands (Melanesia) to the east. Parts of the Coral Sea are very deep. Oceanographers have measured depths to 3 miles (5 km) in some parts.

Many polyps living together in a colony form a single piece of coral. Over the years coral structures grow larger and larger. Their shapes depend on the kind of polyp that formed them. A *sea fan*, for example, is a community skeleton of polyps of just one variety of anthozoan. *Reef-building corals* make enormous underwater ridgelike formations, as new generations of polyps grow on coral left behind by dead polyps. In the warm waters of the Pacific Ocean, coral polyps have built up whole islands. In the warm waters at tropical resorts, such as those in the Caribbean Sea, there are often underwater "trails." Snorkelers and skin divers who follow the underwater trails may observe coral and the many fish that seek the shelter of coral reefs.

Coral polyps reproduce in two ways. Small bumps called *buds* appear on the body of an adult polyp. The buds grow larger. Then they break off from the "parent," attach themselves to the colony, and begin to produce calcium carbonate. Budding increases the size of a coral colony. Polyps also lay eggs. The eggs hatch into free swimming larvae that swim away from the colony, drop to the ocean bottom, and begin to form a new coral formation.

The sea's name comes from the large number of coral atolls and reefs that dot the sea's expanse. One of the largest reefs in the world, the Great Barrier Reef, runs through the Coral Sea, lying more than 100 miles (160 km) out from Australia and stretching about 1,250 miles (2,000 km) along the coast and on into the Gulf of Papua. This ancient reef is approximately 15,000 years old and consists of some 350 species of brightly colored corals. Many kinds of fish, such as grouper, snapper, barracuda, and shark, swim along the reef making it very popular with skin divers and snorkelers. Beautiful beaches washed by the warm Coral Sea waters run along the Australian coast. Two major Australian port cities, Brisbane and Townsville, also lie along that coast. Products such as wool, sugar cane, meat, grain, and minerals flow through these ports.

U.S. warships stopped a Japanese task force in these waters in May 1942, in a decisive World War II battle. U.S. forces were then able to

1

2

3

▲ **An atoll is a ringed reef of coral, enclosing a central lagoon. 1. An atoll forms when coral grows in the warm waters surrounding an island. 2. The coral continues to grow but the island sinks or the sea rises. 3. Once the island has disappeared, the coral reef remains, forming a typical atoll.**

begin to plan their drive toward Japan. An aircraft carrier, the U.S.S. *Coral Sea*, built at the end of World War II, is named for this battle.

▶▶▶▶ **FIND OUT MORE** ◀◀◀◀
Australia; Coral; Great Barrier Reef

CORM

SEE BULB

CORN

The word *corn* means corn-on-the-cob, flavored with salt and butter, to most North Americans. Elsewhere, the plant is called *maize*. Corn is a cereal grass (*grain*) that grows on most continents. (The other five main cereal grasses are rice, wheat, oats, rye, and barley.)

Native Americans learned to cultivate corn thousands of years before Europeans set foot in the New World. Corn became one of the

▼ Native Americans in Virginia planted three crops of corn a year so that it did not all ripen at once.

Native Americans' most important foods. They showed it to Columbus. Native Americans taught the early English colonists how to plant, harvest, and cook several kinds of corn.

Corn plants grow from 2 feet to 20 feet (60 cm to 6 m) high. The corn plant has a central stalk from which long leaves grow. At the top of the plant is the male flower (*tassel*) which produces millions of grains of pollen. Ears grow from the stalk where the leaves join it. Each ear is covered with a special kind of leaf, the *husk*. Inside the husk is the *corncob*. *Cornsilk*, long, thin, hairlike tubes, forms along each corncob. The silk is part of the female flowers. Pollen falls from the tassel and travels through the tubes to fertilize the flowers. Each flower develops into a kernel.

Almost all corn grown in the United States is *hybrid* corn, produced by using pollen from one kind of corn to pollinate another kind. The seeds that result from this special *cross-pollination* have features from both plants. By choosing the "parents" very carefully, experts can produce very useful new kinds of corn. Some hybrid corns, for example, have extra long roots, which help them grow in poor soil. Others have longer, fatter ears than their parents.

Corn kernels provide us with large amounts of valuable carbohydrates, fats, and proteins. Sweet corn, which we often eat as corn-on-the-cob or as canned or frozen corn, is high in vitamin-A content. Corn is an important food for animals, too. Farmers use most of what they raise to feed their cattle, sheep, poultry, and especially hogs.

Corn is processed in different ways to be used in the foods we eat. Kernels are canned or frozen for vegetables. Cornmeal comes from ground kernels. Tamales, corn bread, and some cold cereals are made from cornmeal. Kernels are *refined* (separated into different parts) to obtain many products, called by-products.

▲ The Coral Sea lies in the southern Pacific Ocean, just off the coast of Australia.

The ears of corn we eat today were only an inch (2.5 cm) long in their wild form, hundreds of years ago. By the time Columbus reached the New World the Native Americans had developed corn into the size we know.

▼ Modern corn cobs may be related to a grass, called *Thea sinte,* that grows in Mexico. Its cobs look like small corn cobs.

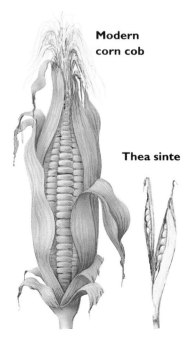

Modern corn cob

Thea sinte

▼ **Some of the many by-products of corn.**

Corn oil comes from the central part of the kernel, or *germ*. Corn oil is used in salad dressing and margarine. Corn oil is also used in cooking, when frying such things as doughnuts or chicken. *Cornstarch*, a white powder, comes from the substances that sur-round the germ of each kernel. Cornstarch thickens gravies and sauces. *Corn syrup* is a liquid used in baking and in making candy.

In addition, corn meal is used in manufacturing adhesives and ply-wood and many soaps and paints contain corn oil. Cornstarch is needed for making drugs, cosmetics, and explosives. Cornstarch is also used to stiffen fabrics and yarns. Husks are sometimes used as a filler material, and stalks may be used for making paper and wallboard.

The United States is the world's leading producer of corn. China is sec-ond. It is the world's third most important cereal crop after wheat and rice. Corn grows in areas that have summer temperatures in the 70s and 80s°F (20s–30s°C). At least 6 to 12 inches (15 to 30 cm) of rainfall are required during the growing season. Rich, well-drained soil is needed.

So much corn is grown in the U.S. Midwest that this region is known as the *corn belt*. States in this area include Nebraska, Kansas, Minnesota, South Dakota, Iowa, Missouri, Illinois, Indi-ana, Wisconsin, and Ohio.

▶▶▶▶ **FIND OUT MORE** ◀◀◀◀
Grains; Native Americans;
Plant Breeding

▼ **Coronado led the first expedition to explore the American Southwest.**

Coronado's Expeditions
1540-1542
— Main route
--- Secondary routes

THE 10 LARGEST U.S. INDUSTRIAL CORPORATIONS (by sales)

1. General Motors
2. Exxon
3. Ford Motor
4. IBM
5. General Electric
6. Mobil
7. Philip Morris
8. Du Pont
9. Chevron
10. Texaco

CORONADO, FRANCISCO (1510–1554)

Francisco Vásquez de Coronado, explorer of the American Southwest, was born in Salamanca, Spain. He went to Mexico in 1535, drawn—like other conquistadors (conquer-ers)—by numerous tales of gold. He soon became governor of a Mex-ican province. Five years later, Coro-nado formed an expedition to seek the legendary Seven Cities of Cibola and to claim new lands for Spain. He led 300 Spanish soldiers and 1,000 Indians northward into what is now Arizona and New Mexico. They found Zuñi villages instead of the golden cities.

Part of the group turned west-ward, becoming the first Europeans to see the Grand Canyon. Coronado and the others crossed the Rio Grande and the Texas Plains. They were the first Europeans to see Amer-ican buffalo (bison). Next, Coronado traveled north to look for Quivira, another "city of gold," but he found only more Native American villages in what is now the state of Kansas.

Failure to find gold made Coro-nado unpopular with the Spanish gov-ernment. His governor's post was taken away in 1544. He later received a small land grant for his services.

▶▶▶▶ **FIND OUT MORE** ◀◀◀◀
Arizona; Cibola, Seven Cities of;
Conquistador; Exploration;
New Mexico

CORONATION

SEE KINGS AND QUEENS

CORPORATION

A corporation is an organization established by a legal process and formed for the purpose of carrying on an activity. Most of the things that

Americans buy and use every day are made by corporations in the United States or abroad. For example, your family's car may have been made by a U.S. corporation such as General Motors, Ford or Chrysler. Other large corporations in the United States today include Exxon, IBM, and Mobil.

Corporations make and sell many kinds of goods and services. Gas and electricity are sold by corporations. Radio and television networks are owned by corporations. Public corporations are formed to govern towns, cities, and schools. The officials who run public corporations are elected by the voters of the area.

A business does not have to be large to be a corporation. Suppose ten people want to join together to make and sell shoes. They need *capital* of 200,000 dollars to begin work. They *invest*, or put up, about 150,000 dollars. This is broken up into small parts, or *shares* of *stock*. To get the 50,000 dollars they still need, they sell shares to other people. The shareholders then own part of the company. To become a corporation, they must ask a state government for a *charter*, or permit, to *incorporate*. The letters "Inc." (for "Incorporated") are then written after the company's name.

The shareholders elect a *board of directors* to manage the business. Each shareholder has as many votes as he or she has shares of stock. One owner can take the place of another by buying the shares of someone else who no longer wants to own shares. Every corporation must obey special laws. A Federal Government agency, the Securities and Exchange Commission, makes rules to govern the sale of stock by the corporation. These rules protect the stockholders.

A corporation is especially helpful in raising money to run a big business. For example, it would be difficult for 10 or 12 people to put up millions of dollars to build and run a railroad. But many thousands of people can invest small sums of money in a corporation to make up the large amount it needs. No matter how large a corporation is, under law it is treated as one individual. This means that the chairperson of the board of directors of the corporation can sign contracts in its name. You can sue a corporation if it does something you think is wrong. But individual persons within a corporation cannot be sued for something done in the name of the corporation.

►►►► **FIND OUT MORE** ◄◄◄◄
Stocks and Bonds

CORROSION

All metals suffer on contact with the environment, usually because they are attacked by oxygen in the air, especially in the presence of moisture. The result of this attack is called *corrosion*. The most common example is rust. The surfaces of iron objects are attacked by both oxygen and water so that a flaky *oxide* of iron is formed. Soon the entire object may be rusted away. Other metals are more resistant, suffering merely *tarnishing*. Here, although the surface of the metal is attacked, the *oxidized* surface layer protects the metal beneath from further attack. Copper and silver are metals that tarnish easily.

▲ Rust is the most familiar form of corrosion. It happens because oxygen and water in the air attack iron to produce a flaky iron compound called iron oxide.

LEARN BY DOING

Take two iron nails and paint one of them. Place both nails in a shallow tray. Put the tray outdoors. After a few days the unpainted iron nail will turn rusty. After a few months rust spots appear on the painted nail.

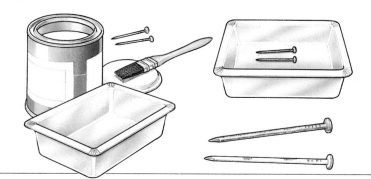

On February 10, 1519, Cortés set sail from Cuba with 508 soldiers, 100 sailors, and 16 horses. His men were armed with flintlock rifles and bows. Despite their small number, this poorly armed force conquered the Aztecs. They did it with military skill, cunning, and determination. Cortés ruled out any possibility of retreat by ordering all his ships to be destroyed.

▲ With help from Indian tribes opposing the Aztecs, Cortés reached the Aztec capital at Tenochtitlán.

▶ The Aztecs were very religious. When Cortés arrived, the Aztecs believed he was a white-skinned god and showered him with gifts.

Air pollution contributes greatly to corrosion, since many gases attack metals even more severely than oxygen. Sulfur dioxide, which is released from domestic and industrial chimneys, is a very bad offender.

Corrosion costs the United States over $5 billion a year. Corrosion-resistant materials like stainless steel as well as paint, varnish, and electroplating can be used to prevent it.

CORTES, HERNANDO (1485–1547)

In March 1519, the Yucatán Indians of Mexico saw white-skinned men arriving in strange ships. Their leader was Captain Hernando Cortés. The goal of this *conquistador* (conquerer) was the conquest of Mexico.

Cortés was born in Medellín, Estremadura, Spain. He began studies in a university but soon left, preferring adventure. He sailed to the New World in 1504 and helped Diego Velásquez conquer Cuba. Velásquez heard about a rich empire in Mexico. He sent Cortés and about 600 men to the unknown country to find gold.

They established the settlement of Veracruz, then traveled inland to Tenochtitlán (later Mexico City).

There they found a dazzling city and a highly developed culture. The natives looked at the Spaniards' ships, cannons, and especially their horses, and thought white-skinned gods had come to their land. Cortés took the ruler, Montezuma, prisoner and ruled the Aztecs through him. Malinche, an Indian princess who was deeply in love with Cortés, aided his conquest by serving as interpreter and guide. Native tribes who feared the Aztecs also helped Cortés. The Aztecs attempted to defeat the Spanish at Otumba in 1521, but Cortés won the battle and as a result Mexico became a Spanish colony.

The king of Spain named Cortés governor of Mexico. Cortés discovered the lower peninsula of California in 1536 and founded a settlement there. Gradually his cruelty and his personal ambition cost him the king's good will. He returned to Spain, where he was coldly received. He died a neglected man.

▶▶▶▶ **FIND OUT MORE** ◀◀◀◀
Aztecs; Conquistador; Mexico

COSMETICS

Cosmetics are substances that people use to make their faces and bodies more attractive. Eyes are thought by many to be prettier when highlighted by makeup. Skin is often softer when creams and lotions are used. Hair looks shiny and stays in place because of cosmetics.

Cosmetics include those that can be seen, such as lipstick, face powder, eye makeup, and nail polish. Others, such as body lotion or hair dressing, are rubbed in.

Most cosmetics are made from a base of fats and oils. These are mixed with water or alcohol and held together by vegetable gums. Colors and perfumes are added. So are other materials that keep the mixture from spoiling. Lipstick is made of castor oil and melted wax with coloring and scent added.

Hand lotions and creams help skin that has been dried out by sun, wind, and water. Special oils are put into these creams.

Cosmetics have been used since the beginning of recorded history. The earliest uses were in religious ceremonies, in which incense and oils were mixed according to old recipes. This was the job of priests or slaves. Cosmetics have been found in ancient Egyptian tombs. The Egyptian queen Cleopatra was famous for her brightly painted face and strange perfume. She bathed in milk to keep her skin soft and beautiful. The Romans were fond of bleaches, dyes, and lotions. Their public baths and barbershops were well stocked with perfumes and oils. Roman women wore chalk and white lead on their faces. They stained their lips and cheeks red.

Until the Crusades, only the very rich in Europe had money to spend on cosmetics. Then returning Crusaders brought perfumes and cosmetics from the East, and the use of beautifiers spread. In the 1500s, Queen Elizabeth I painted her face.

In the United States, pioneer women mixed their own face creams of *lanolin* (grease from sheep's wool)

Deodorant • Nail polish • Hand lotion • Raspberries • Coconut • Chamomile • Wool • Perfume • Cucumber • Rouge • Rose • Lipstick • Lip pencil • Soaps • Hair gel • Shampoo

▲ Some cosmetic products and their natural ingredients.

or beeswax, oil, and water. They washed their faces with buttermilk to remove freckles and colored their lips and cheeks with berry juice.

Until the 1900s, cosmetics were sold only in barbershops and drugstores. Today, the making of cosmetics has become a giant industry. Beauty preparations and *nonallergenic* cosmetics (cosmetics to which no one is allergic) can be bought in department stores, supermarkets, beauty salons, and drugstores, from door-to-door salespersons, or through the mail. A government agency, the Food and Drug Administration, sets rules for ingredients in cosmetics. Since 1976, cosmetics labels must carry a list of all ingredients. Most cosmetics used to be tested on animals, but this practice has decreased due to concern about the suffering of the animals. Today, many cosmetics carry the label "Not tested on animals" on their containers.

▶▶▶▶ **FIND OUT MORE** ◀◀◀◀
Fashion; Makeup; Perfume

COSMIC RAYS

Cosmic rays are tiny particles that travel through space at nearly the speed of light. They are not rays at all. Instead, they are parts of atoms that were torn apart and flung on their high-speed journeys.

▼ Primary cosmic rays are broken down into secondary rays when they pass through the Earth's atmosphere.

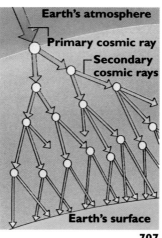

Earth's atmosphere
Primary cosmic ray
Secondary cosmic rays
Earth's surface

COSTA RICA

Capital city
San José (280,000 people)

Area
19,600 square miles (50,700 sq. km)

Population
2,900,000 people

Government
Republic

Natural resources
Coffee, bananas, lumber, gold, hematite, sulfur

Export products
Coffee, bananas, manufactured goods

Unit of money
Colon

Official language
Spanish

Most cosmic rays are produced in *supernovae,* or exploding stars, far removed from our solar system. Some are produced by our own sun. The cosmic rays traveling through space are known as *primary rays*. These rays contain dangerous radiation. Luckily, the magnetic field in our Earth's atmosphere reflects most primary rays.

Some primary rays do penetrate the atmosphere. These rays break up the nitrogen and oxygen atoms in the atmosphere, producing other particles known as *secondary rays.*

Scientists can predict when the number of cosmic rays are at their highest. Space flights usually avoid these peak periods, so that astronauts will be protected from the radiation.

▶▶▶▶ **FIND OUT MORE** ◀◀◀◀
Atmosphere; Atom; Radiation; Radiation Belt; Star

COSTA RICA

Christopher Columbus began his last voyage to the New World in 1502. He sailed along the Caribbean coast of a country where he saw native people wearing golden ornaments and headdresses. He knew he had found another rich land. He named the country Costa Rica, which means "rich coast."

Costa Rica is one of the smallest countries in Central America. It is about as large as New Hampshire and Vermont put together but has many more people.

Costa Rica's shores are washed by the Pacific Ocean on one side and the Caribbean Sea on the other. From hot coastal plains dotted with forests and banana plantations, the land rises sharply up to high, rugged mountains that include many volcanoes. In 1963, the volcano Irazu spilled volcanic ash over much of Costa Rica. The ash poisoned thousands of acres of farmland, destroying many acres of valuable crops.

Most Costa Ricans are of mixed Spanish and native descent. They are called *mestizos*. There are also blacks who are the descendants of slaves brought from the West Indies. More than 90 percent of the population can read and write. More than half of the people are farmers who raise coffee, bananas, cacao, sugarcane, and beans. Costa Rica was the first Central American country to raise coffee, which is its most valuable export. Most Costa Ricans live in the fertile central highlands where days are warm and nights are chilly all year. Rich soil is Costa Rica's chief resource, but minerals, especially gold, are mined in mountains along the Pacific Coast.

San José, the capital and largest city of Costa Rica, is a charming place, with iron grillwork balconies hanging over narrow cobbled streets and beautiful gardens.

Costa Rica was a Spanish colony for about 300 years. It broke away from Spain in 1821 and became

La Cruz
Los Chiles
Papagayo Gulf
GUANACASTE MTS.
Liberia
Cañas
San Juan R.
Frío R.
San Carlos R.
Chirripó R.
Colorado
Caribbean Sea
Santa Cruz
Tempisque R.
Nicoya
Quesada
Grecia
CENTRAL MTS.
Alajuela
Heredia
Puerto Limón
Puntarenas
Grecia
San José
Cartago
Nicoya Gulf
TALAMANCA
Térraba R.
Puerto Quepos
Cerro Chirripó 12,530 ft. 3,819 m.
Dominical
MTS.
General R.
Drake
Neily
Puerto Jiménez
Dulce Gulf
PACIFIC OCEAN

N
W E
S

0   50   100 Miles
0   50   100   150 Kilometers
© 1994 GeoSystems, an R.R. Donnelley & Sons Company

independent in 1838. Since then revolutions have upset the government from time to time, although Costa Rica has been a stable democratic republic for many years.

▶▶▶▶ **FIND OUT MORE** ◀◀◀◀
Central America; Coffee;
Spanish History

COTE D'IVOIRE

When European explorers first visited West Africa, they set up trading posts for ivory in a particular region of the coast. This region became known as the Côte d'Ivoire or Ivory Coast. Today, the country located there is an independent republic about the size of the state of New Mexico. It is on the southern coast of the West African bulge, on the Gulf of Guinea. The Mali Republic and Burkina Faso lie to the north. Guinea and Liberia are its western neighbors, and Ghana lies to the east.

In the Côte d'Ivoire, thick rain forests spread inland from the coastal capital, Abidjan. Farther north, grassy plains, called *savannas*, rise to an area of rolling hills and mountains. The climate is hot and humid in the coastal region and cooler in the north.

The people of the Côte d'Ivoire are called Ivorians. The official language is French, but most people speak one of the more than 60 local African languages. About two-thirds of the people follow African tribal religions. A smaller number of people are Muslims or Christians.

The Côte d'Ivoire has long been one of the most prosperous West African nations. Numerous crops thrive on the fertile soil. Bananas, pineapples, coffee, cocoa, cotton, and palm oil are important products. Rubber and timber (mahogany and other hardwoods) are also valuable sources of income. There are deposits of diamonds, manganese, and other minerals in the ground.

COTE D'IVOIRE

Capital city
Abidjan (1,850,000 people)

Area
124,504 square miles (322,463 sq. km)

Population
12,657,000 people

Government
Multi-party republic

Natural resources
Oil, diamonds, manganese, iron ore, cobalt, bauxite, copper

Export products
Cocoa, coffee, lumber, cotton, fruit, palm oil

Unit of money
Franc of the African Financial Community

Official language
French

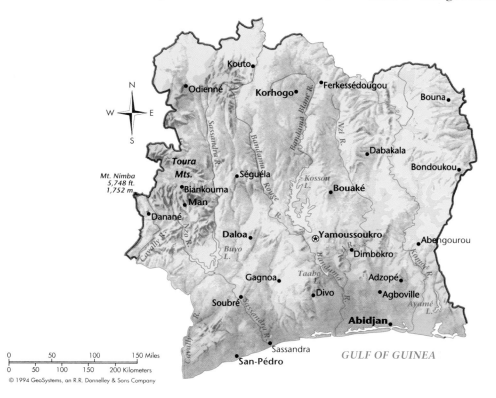

▲ A lagoon near Abidjan, the capital of the Côte d'Ivoire.

▲ **A ripe cotton boll that has split open to reveal fluffy white cotton fibers.**

▼ **Slaves picking cotton on a plantation in the 1800s. The large plantations of the southern states of America relied on cheap labor. The reluctance of these states to give up their slaves was one of the causes of the Civil War.**

Rich fisheries exist along the coast. Among the country's main industries are food and lumber processing, oil refining, assembly of automobiles, textiles, and shipbuilding.

The first Europeans to visit the region of the Côte d'Ivoire were Portuguese explorers in the 1400s. French missionaries and traders arrived in the 1600s. The French claimed the region as a colony of France in 1893. The Côte d'Ivoire gained its independence in 1960. It is governed by a president and his ministers. In 1985, it officially changed its name to Côte d'Ivoire.

▶▶▶▶ **FIND OUT MORE** ◀◀◀◀
Africa

COTTON

One of the most widely used of all plant fibers is cotton, probably the first plant fiber ever to be used by human beings.

The cotton plant is a big-leaf shrub of the mallow family. It grows only within an area from 40 degrees north to 30 degrees south of the equator. (Look at this band on a globe or map.) Cotton seeds are planted in long rows in early spring. A good crop of cotton needs a large amount of fertilizer and must be kept free from weeds. Cutting out weeds by hand with hoes was called *cotton chopping,* but weeds are now controlled by special chemicals.

Yellow blossoms appear on the plant when it is about three feet (90 cm) tall. The blossoms are followed by sticky green capsules, or *bolls,* that grow to the size of a small fist. During the fall, the capsules turn brown and burst open. Inside are many black seeds among the white cotton fibers.

Cotton-picking machines were first used in the 1940s. Before this time, each boll had to be picked by hand. Prior to the Civil War, all the jobs on the cotton plantations in the southern United States, including cotton picking, were done by slaves.

After picking, wagonloads of bolls are carried to a machine called a *gin,* which separates the fibers, seeds, and husks. The fibers are packed into long bales. Each bale weighs about 500 pounds (225 kg). It is wrapped in burlap and bound with metal straps for shipment to spinning mills, where it is made into thread. From this thread a light, hard-wearing cloth is made, used for making garments, furnishings, and other products. Other products are made from the cotton-seeds, fibers, and husks. These include cottonseed oil, margarine, fer-

► An Indian woman spins thread from cotton fibers.

tilizers, cellulose fibers, cardboard, artificial leather, and medicines.

Planters began to grow cotton crops in America after 1620. The cotton gin was invented by Eli Whitney in 1793. The gin made the short-fibered upland cotton easier to process. Cotton was then grown all across the southern United States to what is now California. Other types of cotton grown in the United States are Egyptian and Sea Island cotton. Both have very long fibers.

Cotton growing was severely hurt in the years following 1890 when the *boll weevil* from Mexico began attacking the crops. This insect's grubs ate the cotton plant's buds and made them fall off the plant. The boll weevil still exists today, but now it can be controlled. Some good came out of the boll weevil blight. Farmers turned from one-crop farming to growing several crops and to raising livestock. The new ways of farming, because they were better for the soil, were generally more profitable.

The world's major producers of cotton include the United States, China, India, Pakistan, and Brazil.

▶▶▶▶ **FIND OUT MORE** ◀◀◀◀
Conservation; Slavery; Textile; Whitney, Eli

COUGAR

SEE CAT, WILD

COUNTERFEITING

On his way home from school, a boy found a dollar on the street. He tried to buy some ice cream with it, but the storekeeper refused to accept the dollar because it was a *counterfeit* bill— a worthless copy of a real bill.

"Copy" and "counterfeit" have different meanings. An ordinary copy is not made to cheat anyone. A counterfeit is used to cheat people by making them believe it is genuine, not a copy. Paintings, stamps, and labels for products have been counterfeited. But money has been counterfeited more than anything else.

Only a government is allowed to print and coin money. The government guarantees, or promises, that the money has value and may be used to pay for goods and services. Storekeepers and banks might be afraid to accept bills and coins if a great amount of counterfeit money were in *circulation* (use). People might then lose trust in the money and the government. This could even result in the closing of stores and other places of business. If that happened, the nation's economy could be hurt badly. The U.S. Secret Service—an agency of the Treasury Department—helps prevent this. Each year, the agency seizes millions of dollars in counterfeit money before it can get into circulation. It also prints booklets telling us how to recognize counterfeit money.

Look carefully at a dollar bill. It has many words, pictures, and designs on it. A counterfeiter would have to be a very good artist to copy it exactly. He would have to know how to make and use plates for printing. He would also have to match the colors of ink and use the special kind of paper on which U.S. dollars are printed. Counterfeiters can rarely make a perfect copy of a bill, and so they are usually caught.

▶▶▶▶ **FIND OUT MORE** ◀◀◀◀
Money

▲ A cotton-picking machine harvests cotton bolls.

▲ Part of a counterfeit bill (left) compared with part of a real one. The counterfeit money does not have the same detail as the real money.

COUNTING

SEE NUMBER

COUNTRY MUSIC

SEE POPULAR MUSIC

COUNTY

A county ("borough" in Alaska and "parish" in Louisiana) is a government unit smaller than a state but usually larger than a city or township. The 50 states are divided into more than 3,000 counties.

The word "county" comes from the French word *comte,* or "count." A French county was the estate of a count. The English originally called their counties "shires" but began to use the French word during the 1400s. England is divided into 45 counties. When English colonists came to America, they brought the word "county" and the idea of local government with them.

States do not all have the same number of counties. Delaware has 3, and Texas has 254. Counties are very important in the southern and western parts of the United States. But in New England, where towns are closer together, town and city governments have taken over many county-government jobs and functions.

Each state sets up its own counties, and state laws say what powers the county governments will have. Many counties collect taxes, build and maintain roads, and run schools, parks, hospitals, fire departments, courts, and jails.

State laws decide the form of county government. Many counties are run by a *county board,* an elected group of 2 to 100 people. Other counties are run by a *manager* and a nine-member *council.*

▶▶▶▶ **FIND OUT MORE** ◀◀◀◀
Local Government; State Government

COURT SYSTEM

A court is a room in which a trial takes place. The word "court" can also mean the people who have the right to make the decision in a trial. Some courts have a judge who makes all the decisions. Some have both a judge and a *jury* (a group of people chosen from the citizens at large whose job is to reach a *verdict,* or decision, after hearing facts about both sides of a case). Other courts have a group of judges who take a vote to decide cases.

Most courts have court reporters who take down in shorthand or on a machine every word spoken while court is in session. This is important, particularly when witnesses are giving *testimony* (their knowledge of some of the facts of a case). Before witnesses testify, they must take an *oath*—swear that they will tell the truth. There are often people watching the trial proceedings. Nearly all trials are open to the public.

Two kinds of cases come before

The largest United States county is San Bernardino County, California, at 20,064 square miles (52,000 sq. km). The smallest is Kalawo, Hawaii, at 14 square miles (36 sq. km).

▼ **The city of New York is divided into five counties, called boroughs. Manhattan is the smallest borough in area, covering 34 square miles (88 sq. km). It has the city's tallest buildings.**

courts. In *criminal cases*, a person accused of a crime is *prosecuted*, or tried (taken before a court), to see if he or she did commit the crime. In *civil* cases, two people or groups of people come to court to settle a disagreement between them. One person or group (the *plaintiff*) has filed charges against (*sued*) the other (the *defendant*). The United States has two different court systems—the federal courts and the state courts.

The Federal Court System

Federal courts make judgments in cases having to do with the U.S. Constitution or other federal law. They hear cases in which the United States is suing or prosecuting someone, or some group, or is being sued. They handle disputes between citizens of two different states and disputes involving foreign countries and U.S. citizens. Crimes that happen on ships at sea, called *admiralty cases*, are also brought into federal courts.

Federal courts are set up on three levels. The lowest federal courts are the *district courts*, where most federal cases are heard first. The United States is divided into more than 90 areas. In each area is a district court.

The *Court of Appeals* is the next highest in the federal court system. The Court of Appeals is divided into 11 circuits (areas) that cover all the states, territories, and possessions of the United States. Defendants who are not satisfied with the decision of a district court can *appeal* (take a case to) to the Court of Appeals.

The highest federal court is the *Supreme Court* in Washington, D.C. It reviews cases from the Court of Appeals and from the state supreme courts when questions of federal law are involved. Not every case can be taken to the Supreme Court. The *justices* (judges) of the Supreme Court agree to review only the cases they think involve important legal questions. The Supreme Court has the right to decide that any state or fed-

▲ **This impressive, Grecian style building houses the Supreme Court—the highest federal court in the United States.**

eral law is unconstitutional and must be taken off the books.

The federal system also provides courts for special kinds of cases. The *Court of Claims* handles money claims made against the Federal Government. The *Tax Court* handles cases involving federal tax laws. The *Customs Court* hears cases relating to payment of *duties* (taxes) on imported products. The *Court of Customs and Patent Appeals* reviews some of the cases of the Customs Court as well as decisions made by the Patent Office. The *Court of Military Appeals* reviews cases from the military courts of the U.S. Armed Forces. A military trial is called a *court-martial*.

The State Court System

The state courts handle all cases relating to state laws. The court system of each state is organized differently. In small towns, the lowest courts are usually run by officials called *justices of the peace*. In larger towns or cities, the lowest courts are usually *police courts* or *magistrates' courts*. These courts have judges but no juries. Above them are the state (and sometimes county) *trial courts* with judges and juries. Cases from these courts may be taken to state appeals courts and then, if necessary, to the state's supreme court. States also have special courts for certain types of cases.

The Supreme Court of the United States consists of the chief justice and eight associate justices, all appointed by the President with the advice and consent of the Senate.

Juvenile courts hear cases involving people who are not yet 18 years old. *Probate courts* deal with inheritance cases. Special courts handle divorce trials. Many states set up *small claims courts* for civil cases involving small amounts of money.

▶ ▶ ▶ **FIND OUT MORE** ◀ ◀ ◀

Law; Lawyers and Judges; Patents and Copyrights; Supreme Court; Trial

 ### COUSTEAU, JACQUES-YVES (1910–   )

In the 1930s, the French Navy was testing new diving techniques. A deep-sea diver had to wear a clumsy suit with a metal helmet. He breathed through an air-tube stretching up to the surface. One of the French divers, Jacques Cousteau, wanted to be able to swim freely underwater. He and his team invented *scuba* diving, wearing air-bottles, face masks, and rubber flippers. The breathing apparatus is also called an *aqualung*.

Cousteau proved that people could stay underwater for long periods. He built a seabed research base called Conshelf. He made TV films of underwater life and sailed the world's oceans in his ship, *Calypso*. He also helped develop the bathyscaphe, a deep-diving submersible.

▶ ▶ ▶ **FIND OUT MORE** ◀ ◀ ◀

Scuba Diving

COVERED WAGON

SEE WESTWARD MOVEMENT

COWBOY

A cowboy is a skilled horseman who helps care for cattle on a ranch. People everywhere in the world know about the cowboys of the North American West. Just as famous are the *gauchos*—the cowboys of South America, and the *vaqueros*—the cowboys of Mexico. "Buckaroo," another word for "cowboy," comes from the Mexican word *vaquero*.

The life of a cowboy in the early days of the West was not always as adventurous and exciting as you might imagine from a Western movie or a television show. It was often dull and dreary. Even today, with all the modern inventions, cowboys must work long hours in all kinds of weather at difficult jobs.

Old-time cowboys had to spend many lonely weeks on the plains. Their food was bad. Their pay was low. They often faced danger. They always had to work very hard. But the job cowboys did was very important. They helped in the development of the modern United States. The people in the growing U.S. cities needed meat. This meat came from the cattle that the cowboys tended.

Cattle in the North American West grazed on open range, grassland not closed in by fences. The cattle could wander anywhere to find food. Cowboys patrolled the range to protect the cattle and to make sure the cattle

---

> **Three of Jacques Cousteau's films about sea life have won Academy Awards.**

▼ **Jacques Cousteau, French explorer of the underwater world. He is shown here in his underwater laboratory.**

did not wander too far. They rounded up strays that got lost. When the cattle ate all the grass or drank all the water on one part of the range, cowboys led them to grass or water somewhere else.

Roundup time came every spring and fall. The cowboys gathered all their cattle together in a big herd. A herd often included thousands of cattle. The cowboys counted the cattle and branded the calves. A *brand* is a mark burned on the side of an animal to show who owns it. Cowboys caught cattle and held them for branding with long ropes called *lariats* or *lassos*. Cowboys say that a strong rope and a good horse are the two things they need most.

A cattle drive began when the fall roundup and branding were finished. Cowboys took the cattle they were going to sell to the nearest *railhead*, a town with a railroad station. The cattle drive was the most difficult of the cowboy's tasks. It meant guiding the huge herd of cattle hundreds of miles across open range from the ranch to the railhead. The cattle had to be protected and kept from straying, and there was always danger that the herd might be frightened into a *stampede*— a wild run. The cowboys had to work long hours each day for several weeks to make sure that the cattle made the trip safely. At the railhead, the owner sold his herd to cattle buyers from the East, and the cowboys received their pay for the drive. They often spent all their money celebrating the end of the cattle drive.

Many early cowboys who helped shape North America were blacks. It was unusual in those days for whites and blacks to work together as equals, but on the open range, with so much hard work to be done, any man who did his part was accepted. No one had time to worry about the color of his skin.

Ten-gallon hat

Bandanna

Rifle

Western saddle

Boots Spurs Chaps

The modern West has no open ranges. All the land belonging to a ranch is now surrounded by fences. Cattle drives are no longer necessary. A railroad station is near every cattle ranch, and cattle are shipped to the station by truck. But cowboys still have plenty of work. Cattle must still be rounded up and branded. Modern cowboys still ride horses, but they also use helicopters, jeeps, motorcycles, and short-wave radios. Cowboys are proud of their skills. They have contests, called *rodeos*, with each other to see who is best at riding, roping, and other skills.

◄ **The clothes worn by a cowboy had to be hard-wearing and suitable for a life on the dusty prairie.**

Bill Pickett, a black cowboy on the famous 101 Ranch in Oklahoma, is credited with inventing the art of steer wrestling, or bulldogging.

▼ **An oil painting by Charles M. Russell, called *Cowboys Roping a Steer*. It was painted in 1897.**

▶▶▶▶ **FIND OUT MORE** ◄◄◄◄
Cattle; Ranching; Rodeo; Westward Movement

COYOTE

The coyote is a wild dog of North America. They have brown coats touched with black and gray sprinkles.

▲ Coyotes produce their howls and barks at dusk and dawn. All the coyotes nearby join in.

For a long time the coyote has been the symbol of all that is cowardly and sneaky in animals. When sheep first appeared on Western ranches, coyotes were such a danger that some states offered rewards for coyote scalps.

▶ A whooping crane (top) has a giant wingspread of about 90 inches (2.3 m). It is the largest crane in North America and is very rare. The sandhill crane (below) is more common.

They have pointed ears and noses and bushy tails. Coyotes also have strong voices, as anyone who has heard their evening "concert"—a series of howls and sharp barks—will tell you. Fully grown coyotes stand about 21 inches (53 cm) high at the shoulder and weigh about 30 pounds (14 kg). They can run a long time at 30 miles (48 km) an hour while chasing prey.

The original habitat of the coyote was the Great Plains of the United States. The animal often appeared in the myths and legends of the Native Americans of the Plains as a clever trickster. The coyote roamed this area from the flatlands to the *timberline* (the height above which no trees grow) of mountains. The range of the coyote has expanded to new territory from Costa Rica to Alaska, and east all the way into New England.

Coyote young, called pups, are born in the spring, in a *den* or small cave. The usual litter is five or six. The father helps rear the pups. He delivers food to the den entrance. By autumn the young have to find territories and food of their own.

Coyotes are *carnivores* (meat-eaters). People have always blamed coyotes for hunting sheep and cattle. But recent studies have shown that coyotes do more good than harm. They eat rabbits, gophers, rats, and other crop-destroying rodents. They are fast enough to catch jackrabbits, which eat the grass sheep need.

Coyotes that live near suburban areas and cities have sometimes bred with tame dogs to produce *coydogs*, which resemble both the wild coyote and the tame dog.

▶▶▶▶ **FIND OUT MORE** ◀◀◀
Dog; Mammal; Prairie

CRAB

SEE CRUSTACEAN

CRANE

Cranes are long-legged, long-necked birds. They are known for their loud cry that can be heard for miles and for the high-jumping dance they perform during their mating season. Cranes fly in large flocks, with their long necks pointing straight forward and their stiltlike legs pointing straight back. Many species are found throughout the world, but no cranes live in South America, Malaysia, or the small islands of the Pacific. Cranes are "old" birds. Fossils from France, Greece, and the United States show that birds like them were flying around about 60 million years ago.

Two kinds of cranes live in North America. One is the common *sandhill* crane. Its feathers are gray, and on its forehead is a bright red bald spot. Most sandhills live west of the Mississippi River. In winter they live in southern California, Mexico, and Central America. In summer they nest from Michigan west to Washington state, and as far south as Colorado. Many of these cranes spend the summer in Canada, where they nest as far north as Baffin Island. A few live in the marshes of Florida and southern Georgia.

The second North American member of this family is the *whooping* crane, whose voice sounds like a trumpet. Its feathers are white, except for a few black ones on the wing tips. Its face is bright red. Whooping cranes are large birds, over 5 feet (1.5 m) tall and with a wingspread of 90 inches (2.3 m) or more.

Whooping cranes summer in part of the Northwest Territories of Canada. They winter on the Texas coast, in the area now called the Aransas Wildlife Refuge. Whooping cranes were numerous in the 1800s, but fewer than 200 are living today, partly because people killed thousands of these birds for food. Whooping cranes are in danger of dying out, so laws in North America have made it illegal to kill them.

Cranes are marsh or water birds. They eat mainly berries, fruits, roots, and fish. Sometimes they eat mice, insects, snakes, and snails.

Cranes have several close relatives in North America. These include the ducklike *coot,* an expert swimmer and diver, whose body is gray and black and whose tail is white; the *common* and *purple gallinules,* who usually feed at the edges of lakes; and several species of *rails,* all of whom fly poorly, but who run swiftly and silently through tall grass to escape enemies.

▶ ▶ ▶ ▶ **FIND OUT MORE** ◀ ◀ ◀ ◀
Bird; Stork

CRANE, STEPHEN (1871–1900)

Stephen Crane was an American author. His most famous novel, *The Red Badge of Courage* (1895), describes the thoughts and experiences of a young Union soldier during the Civil War in America.

Crane was born in Newark, New Jersey. He studied at Lafayette College and Syracuse University, where he was a catcher on the baseball team. He then worked in New York City as a newspaper reporter. His first novel, *Maggie, a Girl of the Streets* (1893), tells the story of brutal life in the slums. Crane, along with other authors of the time, developed a way of writing called *naturalism,* using detailed realism and factual description, which he used to tell the reader his ideas about life. Crane thought that people were all victims of chance.

Crane became a foreign correspondent for several newspapers. He reported the war between the Greeks and Turks and, later, the Spanish-American War. He told about one of his own scary experiences in a short story, "The Open Boat"—the tale of a shipwrecked expedition to Cuba. This short story, and several others that Crane wrote, are important in the history of U.S. fiction. Crane showed later writers how to use the short-story form effectively.

Crane wrote two important books of poetry, *The Black Riders* and *War Is Kind.* He wrote in free verse and in a style used later by other poets. He developed tuberculosis during his travels and died in Germany at the age of 28.

▶ ▶ ▶ ▶ **FIND OUT MORE** ◀ ◀ ◀ ◀
Literature; Novel; Poetry; Short Story

CRATER

SEE METEOR; VOLCANO

▲ **One of the most handsome cranes, the crowned crane of southern Africa.**

▲ **Stephen Crane, U.S. author and poet, introduced a new realism to fiction.**

▲ **A Cree woman from Quebec, Canada, carrying a bowl of fresh blueberries. The Cree of the United States moved south from Canada.**

▼ **A Cree summer encampment. The teepees were covered with bark and could be moved by canoe.**

CREDIT CARD

A woman knows that on New Year's Day she will receive a $1,000 bonus from her employer. In the meantime she sees a $250 watch that would make a good Christmas present for her husband.

Not long ago this would have been a real problem. The woman would have missed out on buying the watch because her money was arriving too late for Christmas.

Credit cards, which are now very common, solved the problem. They offer people the chance to buy something now and pay for it later. Many people do all their shopping with credit cards, and carry little or no cash with them.

The woman in the example could have paid for the watch with a credit card. The credit card company would pay the store $250 and then send a bill for that amount to the woman. The woman's bill would probably arrive after her bonus, so she could pay it easily.

Some large oil companies and some large stores issue credit cards. These cards can be used only at their service station or store. Banks and travel companies issue cards that can be used at a wide range of stores. These credit companies often charge stores a fee for their service. They may also charge their customers a small annual card fee.

A credit card purchase is like a loan. The person "borrows" the amount of the purchase and promises to pay it back when the bill is sent. Some credit card companies allow customers to pay back only part of their bill. But these customers must pay a *financial charge* or *interest* on the unpaid amount that can be quite expensive.

A credit card has the person's name and his or her personal account number. This information can be read by computer. On the back of the card is an example of the person's signature as a further form of identification.

▶▶▶▶ **FIND OUT MORE** ◀◀◀◀
Banks and Banking

CREES

A large tribe of Algonkian-speaking Native Americans, the Cree, once wandered freely through the woodlands of eastern and central Canada. A small number of Cree moved into the United States in the 1700s. They became buffalo hunters. A Cree hunter could move either by land or by water to find food for himself and his family. If animals were plentiful, he killed deer, caribou, moose, or rabbit. If animals grew scarce, he took to his canoe to fish.

The Cree knew their way around the rivers, and they willingly guided European explorers. According to white fur trappers who knew them, the Cree were generous, good-natured, and friendly. They were also good bargainers when it came to trading furs for pots and utensils.

Cree men wore tight leather leggings up to the hip, short leather pants, and moccasins. Cree women wore knee-length garments made of skins, pulled in at the waist with a belt. They added detachable sleeves in cold weather.

Smallpox, introduced by the white settlers, killed many Cree. About 33,000 Cree live today on reservations set up in Manitoba and other Canadian provinces.

▶▶▶▶ **FIND OUT MORE** ◀◀◀◀
Algonkian; Native Americans

CREEKS

The Creeks included several tribes whose members spoke similar languages of the Muskogean family. The Creeks lived in about 50 permanent towns in the present-day states of Georgia, Alabama, and Florida.

Creek women raised corn, beans, squash, and pumpkins. Creek men hunted deer, bear, beaver, and squirrel. The warriors made bows and arrows and blowguns, and they later used rifles. The tribes saved part of each harvest in public storerooms in case of poor crops. Each town provided passing travelers with food. The leaders of all the towns met each year to discuss common problems.

In each town, four public buildings—two for leaders, one for warriors, and one for young people—were built around a public square. In the square was the *chunkey yard,* where young men played the ball game now called lacrosse or shot arrows at a pennant hung from the top of a pole. The wooden houses of the townspeople spread out from the square.

One Creek tribe, the Red Sticks, fought against the United States in 1813 and 1814. The Red Sticks lost, and all Creek tribes were forced to give up much of their land. Whites took the rest of their land in the 1830s, and the Creeks were marched to Indian Territory (now Oklahoma). Nearly half the people died on the trip. Today, about 20,000 Creeks live in northeastern Oklahoma.

▶ ▶ ▶ ▶ **FIND OUT MORE** ◀ ◀ ◀ ◀
Jackson, Andrew; Lacrosse; Native Americans; Trail of Tears; War of 1812

CRETE

SEE GREECE

CRICKET

Cricket is a popular sport in many nations, especially Great Britain and the Commonwealth. It is played mainly by men but is growing in popularity among women.

A cricket ball is slightly smaller than a baseball but weighs a little more. The wooden bat measures a maximum 38 inches (96.5 cm) long by 4¼ inches (10.8 cm) wide. About two-thirds of the length is the broad, flat *blade* (striking surface); the rest is a narrower, cylindrical handle.

A cricket team has 11 players. When one team is batting (each player has a turn to bat), one member of the other team bowls (somewhat like a baseball pitcher) while the other 10 field. An important fielder is the *wicket-keeper.* He stands behind the wicket at which the bowler aims (just like standing behind the plate in baseball). A cricket *inning* is complete when every person on the batting team has had a turn at bat, or when the captain of the batting team decides that his team has scored enough runs. Some matches (games) consist of one innings per team; others, notably *test matches* (played between countries over five days), have two innings per team.

A cricket match is played on a grassy field called a *pitch.* In the center of the pitch, 22 yards (20.1 m) apart, stand two *wickets.* Each wicket is 9 inches (23 cm) wide and consists of three upright *stumps*

▲ A cricket match in 1740. Modern-style bats did not come into use until the 1800s.

King Edward IV of England declared cricket illegal in 1477 because his soldiers played the game instead of practicing archery. Nearly 300 years later, cricket was legally declared "an honorable sport."

◀ The Creeks often decorated their pottery with abstract designs of the sun.

▼ Cricket requires great concentration for both batsmen and fielders alike.

▲ In cricket the ball is bowled overarm. Fast bowlers gain speed by running up to the wicket before delivering the ball.

▼ The batsman in cricket has to try to score as many runs as possible.

(sticks) 28 inches (71 cm) high. Two small sticks called *bails* rest on top of the stumps.

Two batsmen play at the same time. The one who faces the bowler is "on strike." Bowling is rather like throwing overhand, except that the bowler runs up and must keep his arm straight. He bowls from one wicket while the batsman on strike defends the other. Bowlers try either to knock the bails off the batsman's wicket or to make him strike the ball so that it is caught by a fielder before it touches the ground. In either case the batsman is out. Batsmen may also be out if they block the bowler's ball with their body, if they knock the bails off with their bat or a part of their body, or if they are run out (see below). Two umpires adjudicate (act as judge).

A run is made when the batsman hits the ball hard enough that he and the non-strike batsman can both run to their opposite wickets. A run may also be made if the bowler is guilty of some infringement (for example, bowls too wide of the stumps). A *bye* occurs when the batsman misses the ball, the wicket-keeper fails to stop it, and it goes far enough for the batsmen to have time to swap ends. A batsman scores four runs if he has hit the ball so that it goes over the pitch's *boundary,* and six if it does so without first bouncing.

If the fielders throw in the ball so that the wickets are knocked over while a batsman is in the middle of making a run and has not reached the wicket, that batsman is out (*run out*). The team with the highest total of runs wins the game.

Cricket probably developed from bat and ball games that were played in England as long ago as the 1300s. The official rules were not written down until 1744. The first international (*test*) match was played between England and Australia in 1877.

CRIME

All countries make rules, or *laws,* which forbid certain types of behavior. A person who breaks the laws by stealing, for example, has committed a crime and may be punished for that action.

In ancient times, when the first part of the Bible was written, the *Mosaic Code,* also called the *Ten Commandments,* provided laws for people to follow. The Mosaic Code has survived as the basic concept of right and wrong for 4,000 years. "Thou shalt not kill, thou shalt not steal" are laws that still hold true in modern times.

Attitudes to crime do not always stay the same. Laws may be changed as society develops. The definition of crime also varies from country to country. In Muslim countries, a man can have several wives. But in the United States, having more than one wife or husband at a time is a crime called *bigamy.*

Some crimes, however, have always been considered more serious than others. In the United States, serious crimes are called *felonies.* They are usually punished by imprisonment but in some states, certain felonies may be punished by death. Some of the most serious felonies are murder (intentionally killing a person), armed robbery (stealing with the use of a gun or other weapon), assault (attacking a person with the purpose of injury), and arson (intentionally setting a fire). The crime of *treason* (an act of betraying your country) is usually punished by life

▼ In England in the 1800s, criminals called *highwaymen* robbed stage coaches.

▲ If you were convicted of a crime in England from 1788 to 1868 you could be sent to Australia as punishment.

imprisonment, but during war it may be punished by death. *Rape* and other forms of sexual assault are serious crimes.

Other serious felonies are *forgery* (signing another person's name with intent to cheat), *counterfeiting* (printing fake money or other papers), and *embezzlement* (taking people's money, entrusted to your care, for your own use).

Less serious crimes are called *misdemeanors*. Punishment for these offenses is a fine or imprisonment for less than one year. Minor traffic offenses and public drunkenness are sometimes misdemeanors.

In the United States, a person accused of a serious crime has certain rights guaranteed by the *Bill of Rights*, the first ten amendments to the Constitution. These rights include: 1. the right to a fair trial; 2. the right to a trial by jury; 3. the right to a *lawyer*, a person who has studied law and can represent the accused in court (if the accused is too poor to pay for a lawyer, the court appoints one for him); 4. the right to keep silent and not testify against oneself; and 5. the right not to be tried twice for the same crime, even if new evidence is later found.

A person is considered innocent under U.S. law unless proved guilty beyond a reasonable doubt. In a criminal case, the *prosecutor*, a lawyer who works for the government, must prove the guilt of the accused, who is called the *defendant*.

Reasons for Crime

Crime is committed for many differ-

ent reasons. Some people steal because they cannot afford to buy the thing they desire. Cars are often stolen because they are symbols of wealth, and they also make it easier to escape from the scene of a crime.

"Organized crime," often called the "underworld," is a name for organizations of criminals who run illegal operations, including selling dangerous drugs. Drugs have caused a frightening increase in crime. Addicts are sometimes so desperate to buy their drugs that they commit crimes for the money.

Many crimes are committed by people who live in the poor areas of large cities. They may come from broken homes, have very little money, and few job prospects. They may feel that there is no way of getting what they want except through crime. These people are often the victims of crime, too. Society can help prevent crime by combating poverty, by improving schools and education, by cleaning up slums, and by providing decent housing and jobs for all people.

A crime is committed when people *defraud*, or cheat, other people in business. People who do not declare all their income on their tax returns are also committing a crime. These sorts of crimes are known as "white-collar" crimes.

Factories that belch out smoke, causing pollution that can kill people, and pharmaceutical companies who distribute products that find their way into the illegal drugs market, are committing the kind of crimes that can often go unpunished.

Every citizen should be aware of the law and one's rights under the law. Citizens should know how justice is administered in the community and nation. They should be aware of crime. Only in this way can they protect themselves and their society.

▶ ▶ ▶ ▶ **FIND OUT MORE** ◀ ◀ ◀ ◀
Bill of Rights; Citizenship; Court System; Juvenile Delinquency; Law

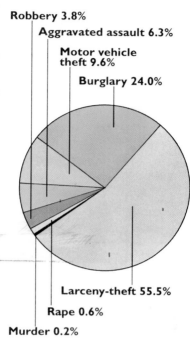

▼ The most common reported crimes committed in the United States.

Robbery 3.8%
Aggravated assault 6.3%
Motor vehicle theft 9.6%
Burglary 24.0%
Larceny-theft 55.5%
Rape 0.6%
Murder 0.2%

The highest amount of damages ever sought was in a case in 1971 in which Mr. Walton Bader asked for $675,000,000,000,000 from General Motors for polluting the atmosphere in all 50 states. As that sum was then equal to ten times the U.S. national wealth, it is unlikely that Mr. Bader expected to get what he asked for.

▲ Florence Nightingale and her team of nurses saved many lives during the Crimean War. Deaths dropped from around 50 percent of the wounded to around 2 percent.

▼ The British light cavalry rode to almost certain death at the Battle of Balaklava during the Crimean War. The poet Lord Tennyson commemorated the event in his poem, "The Charge of the Light Brigade."

CRIMEAN WAR

About 500,000 soldiers were wounded or killed in the Crimean War, often called the "war of errors." The war is often best remembered for a nurse who treated the wounded and for a dangerous charge into battle by some British cavalrymen.

The war started in 1854 because of some misunderstandings over control of land. Russia fought on one side against Great Britain, France, and Turkey. Sardinia later joined those against Russia. Most of the war was fought on the large peninsula of Crimea, which pokes into the Black Sea from the Russian mainland.

The nurse whom the war made famous was Florence Nightingale. She is said to have started modern nursing. She did such a good job of taking care of the wounded British soldiers that she became a national heroine in England.

The famous cavalry charge was at the Battle of Balaklava on October 25, 1854. A brigade of nearly 700 British cavalrymen obediently followed their leaders' unwise orders and charged straight into the fire of Russian cannon. Only 195 cavalrymen lived through this dreadful massacre. However, Russia

lost the battle. Alfred, Lord Tennyson, an Englishman, wrote a poem, "The Charge of the Light Brigade," which made this event famous as an example of the British soldier's absolute devotion to his duty.

Historians say that the generals on both sides in this war made many errors. These mistakes cost the lives of many soldiers. The war ended when Russia finally gave in. The four countries that took part in the start of the war finally signed a treaty in 1856 and agreed to respect each others' territories.

▶▶▶▶ **FIND OUT MORE** ◀◀◀◀
Nightingale, Florence; Tennyson, Alfred

CROATIA

Croatia is located along the Adriatic Sea in the Balkan region of southeast Europe. It was one of the six republics that made up Yugoslavia. It is bordered by Slovenia and Hungary to the north, Serbia to the east, and Bosnia and Herzegovina to the south.

A narrow strip of Croatia extends down the Adriatic coast. The Dinaric Alps, a barren mountain range, runs along this coast. The Croats living there have traditionally earned their income from olive growing, fishing, and tourism. Recently, industries have developed the region's coal, bauxite, and hydroelectric power.

Zagreb, Croatia's capital, is located in the flatter inland region. Farms on the fertile land there produce corn, wheat, sugar beets, and grapes.

The Croats became Christian in 803, and remain devout Roman Catholics. In 1091, Croatia fell under Hungarian, and later Austrian, control, which lasted for 800 years. The end of World War I saw the end of the Austro-Hungarian empire. In 1918, Croatia joined Serbia, Macedonia, and Montenegro to form what became known as Yugoslavia.

But there were important differences between the states. Croats and Serbs both speak Serbo-Croatian, but Croats use the Roman alphabet and Serbs use the Cyrillic alphabet, like Russians. The Serbs are members of the Eastern Orthodox religion, another difference from Croatia. The Croats felt that Serbia had too much power in Yugoslavia.

After Germany defeated Yugoslavia in 1941, Croatia declared its independence. Ustasha, a fascist group supported by Germany, ruled Croatia. Many Serbs and opponents of Ustasha were executed.

After World War II, Croatia again became part of Yugoslavia, which had become a Communist country. But differences with Serbia again rose to the surface. By the late 1980s, Croatia and other republics felt that Serbia had too much power.

Croatia declared its independence in 1991. Serbia invaded Croatian areas where large numbers of Serbs lived. They reminded people of Ustasha's crimes in the 1940s, and claimed that Serbs could not find safety in an independent Croatia. Serbia *annexed* (took control of) several regions.

In 1992, Croatian forces were fighting in neighboring Bosnia and Herzegovina. Croats living in that republic were forced off their land to make way for Serbian settlements. Many Croatians, including women and children, were brutally murdered.

▶▶▶▶ **FIND OUT MORE** ◀◀◀◀
Bosnia and Herzegovina; Slovenia; Yugoslavia

CROCKETT, DAVY
(1786–1836)

David Crockett was born in Limestone, Tennessee. He fought under Andrew Jackson in the campaign against the Creeks during the War of 1812 and rose to the rank of colonel. He was elected to the Tennessee legislature in 1823. Three years later, he accepted a dare to run for Congress and, to his surprise, he was elected. He served three terms, becoming a beloved figure in Washington, D.C., because of his backwoods costumes and tall stories.

CROATIA

Capital city
Zagreb (1,175,000 people)

Area
21,829 square miles (56,537 sq. km)

Population
4,600,000 people

Government
Republic

Natural resources
Petroleum, bauxite, grains, sugar beets, grapes, olives

Export products
Oil and oil-related products, chemical products, ships, textiles, machinery

Unit of money
Croatian Dinar

Official language
Serbo-Croatian

▲ **Davy Crockett, a hero of the U.S. frontier and subject of many a tall tale.**

▲ Oliver Cromwell (above), the Lord Protector, and his banner (below).

Across
1. one of the seasons
5. 3rd person singular of *to be*
6. sharp tool
7. Cincinnati team
10. the smallest unit of an element
12. instead
13. I and at least one other person
14. the European country whose capital is Stockholm

Down
1. gentlemen
2. to put into service
3. it supports a sail
4. formerly (abbr.)
8. challenge
9. the end of a prayer
11. to be in debt
12. exclamation of pain

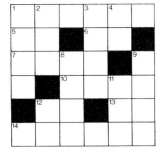

Popular songs and plays were written about him. *The Crockett Almanacks,* first published in 1835, gained worldwide fame.

Crockett lost the election of 1835 because of his opposition to President Jackson's land and Native American policies. He went to Texas to aid the independence movement there and died on March 6, 1836, defending the Alamo.

▶▶▶▶ **FIND OUT MORE** ◀◀◀◀
Alamo; Jackson, Andrew; War of 1812

CROCODILE

SEE ALLIGATORS AND CROCODILES

CROMWELL, OLIVER (1599–1658)

Oliver Cromwell governed Britain from 1649 to 1658. These nine years were the only period in British history when the nation had no king or queen. Britain was proclaimed a republic, called the Commonwealth.

Cromwell was elected to Parliament in 1628 and again in 1640. While in Parliament, he joined the Roundheads, who opposed King Charles I. Charles wanted no interference from Parliament (the people's elected representatives); he believed in the *divine right of kings,* that monarchs were responsible only to God, and that their subjects should therefore obey them without question.

In 1642, a civil war began between the Roundheads (who got their name because they cut their hair very short) and the Cavaliers (who supported the King). As lieutenant-general of the army, Cromwell showed his military genius by building the Roundhead army into a great fighting force. He led the army in many victorious

battles. After the war, Cromwell sat on the court that tried King Charles for treason, and was one of the signers of the King's death warrant. Supported by the Roundhead army, Cromwell became governor of Britain. He was made Lord Protector in 1653.

Cromwell granted religious freedom to the Puritans, Quakers, and Jews. He began as a great supporter of the people. But everyone was confused in the period after the civil war, and Cromwell met many problems. He had his own troubles with Parliament. For a time, he even locked up its meeting place. He was very cruel in putting down revolutions in Ireland and Scotland.

When Cromwell died, his son Richard (1626–1712) became Lord Protector. But where his father had been strong, Richard was weak. He had to resign after a few months, and the son of Charles I was crowned Charles II in 1660.

▶▶▶▶ **FIND OUT MORE** ◀◀◀◀
Charles, Kings of England; English History; Parliament

CROSSWORD PUZZLE

People in all parts of the world have enjoyed solving puzzles of various kinds for centuries. Among the most popular are crossword puzzles. They appear in daily and weekly newspapers, in magazines, and in books that have nothing but crossword puzzles in them. Special dictionaries have even been created to help the solver.

To work a crossword puzzle, a person must guess the correct words from printed clues, and then put the letters of these words into a pattern of numbered squares.

To solve the crossword puzzle on this page, copy the pattern on a blank sheet of paper. Draw a large square on the paper and divide the square into 36 smaller squares by drawing 5 evenly spaced lines both across and down. Number the squares as shown—each number marks the beginning of a word—but be sure to leave room for the letters of the words. Shade in the dark squares, which help you see where words begin and end.

Now solve the puzzle on your own sheet. The completed puzzle is printed on page 726 but don't peek until you have finished!

▶ ▶ ▶ ▶ **FIND OUT MORE** ◀ ◀ ◀ ◀
Word Games

CROWN JEWELS

Crown jewels are collections of pieces of jewelry worn or carried by rulers. These jewels have been passed down from one monarch to another for hundreds of years. It is impossible to state the worth of crown jewels in dollars, because of their great historic and symbolic value. Some of the world's greatest gems are found in these collections.

The *crown* is the official sign of a ruler's power. There are two general styles. One is an open headband with designs and jewels set in. The other is the closed crown with arched pieces of metal over the top of the head. Crown-jewel collections also may include *scepters,* ornate rods that monarchs carry on special occasions, and *orbs,* jeweled spheres in which crosses are mounted.

Crowns differ from country to country and from age to age. Byzantine emperors wore either a closed crown or a high pyramid cap covered by pearls and jewels. The Iron Crown of Lombardy is said to contain a nail from the Cross on which Jesus was crucified. Napoleon carried this crown when he was made king of Italy in 1805.

The Austrian Imperial crown, dated 1602, is pure gold, set with

diamonds. This crown, which sat on the heads of several rulers of the Hapsburg (Habsburg) family, is banded top and bottom with pearls. On the very top is a large sapphire.

The Scottish crown was originally a gold band set with large gems and pearls. In 1707, the Scots were afraid the English would take their crown jewels to England. They secretly hid them in Edinburgh Castle and then forgot about them. They were discovered 110 years later. Today, the jewels are on display in Edinburgh.

Henry V of England wore his crown on top of his helmet at the Battle of Agincourt in 1415. While Oliver Cromwell ruled England, there was no king. At that time most of the crown jewels were broken down, melted, and sold. Later, some were bought again and reset.

In the 17th century, the royal goldsmith was put to work on a coronation crown for Charles II, called "St. Edward's Crown." The present Queen Elizabeth, Queen Victoria, and other monarchs used it for their coronations.

The British crown jewels include orbs, scepters, swords, bracelets, *amulets* (charms), and the royal spoon, as well as crowns. They are used on ceremonial occasions to indicate the ruler's various powers and responsibilities. Today, the crown jewels are owned not by the ruler but by the British people. They are displayed in the Tower of London.

▶ ▶ ▶ ▶ **FIND OUT MORE** ◀ ◀ ◀ ◀
Kings and Queens

▲ **The crown of St. Stephen, part of the Hungarian royal regalia. According to tradition, it was given to Stephen (about 975–1038) by the Pope as a reward for having converted so many pagans to Christianity.**

▲ **The British Imperial State Crown is worn by the monarch of the United Kingdom on state occasions, for example, the annual speech to the British Parliament.**

CROWS

Raven

Rook

Magpie

▲ The crow family is a very large one, containing many different types of birds.

S	U	M	M	E	R
I	S		A	X	
R	E	D	S		A
S		A	T	O	M
	O	R		W	E
S	W	E	D	E	N

Answer to puzzle, page 724

If you have ever traveled in the country, you have probably seen flocks of large, jet-black birds in fields or resting in tall trees. These birds are probably crows. Their loud, shrill "caw, caw" cry can be heard a long way as they warn each other of danger or tell of a new supply of food. Crows are found in all parts of the world except New Zealand. Birds of the crow family include rooks, ravens, jays, jackdaws, and magpies.

Although crows generally favor farmlands and woods, they have adapted to many different kinds of environments, including noisy, crowded cities. They are intelligent birds that can be tamed and can learn to imitate human sounds. Crows eat almost anything—vegetables, fruits, insects, and small animals.

Rooks are large crows with a whitish base to their bills. *Ravens* are even bigger and have a strong, large bill. There are some very famous ravens that live in the Tower of London, England. According to Greek myth, ravens used to be white. However, one day a raven told the god Apollo that the nymph Coronas was deceiving him. Apollo killed the nymph but hated the bird that had told him of her deceit so much he painted it black. *Jays* are smallish birds of the crow family. They have various colors. The Blue jay is very well known. *Jackdaws* are also quite small. They are well known for stealing shiny objects such as coins.

▶ ▶ ▶ ▶ **FIND OUT MORE** ◀ ◀ ◀ ◀
Bird

CRUSADES

In the 1000s and the 1300s, large groups of people traveled to the Middle East. They were Christians fighting wars to win control of the Holy Land from the Muslims. Their journeys were called *Crusades*. The word comes from the Latin word meaning "cross." Almost all soldiers of the European armies sewed crosses on their clothing as a sign of their promise to win the Holy Land.

Palestine was important to Christians as the land of Jesus. To the Muslims, Palestine was the land where many of their prophets, like Abraham and Moses, had lived. The Muslims controlled the land and held rich trade routes there. These wars were bitter and bloody.

Wars between Christians and Muslims actually began long before the Crusades. The Muslims had conquered Italy, Sicily, and Spain, but by the time of the First Crusade, they had been pushed from Italy and Sicily, and they were quickly losing Spain. Arab Muslims had also conquered Jerusalem in the 600s. They allowed Christians to visit the holy places. But after Turkish Muslims took Jerusalem in 1071, they did not allow Christian visitors. All of this helped to bring about the First Crusade.

The First Crusade (1096–1099) is said to have been led by a preacher, Peter the Hermit. He took bands of ordinary people on this crusade. They headed for Constantinople (now Istanbul, Turkey), the capital of the Byzantine Empire. Most of these people starved or were killed by the Turks. But they were followed by armies of knights, mostly from France. They marched or took ships to Asia Minor. They met there in 1097 and started toward Jerusalem. On the way they fought many bloody battles. They captured Jerusalem in 1099, and most of the crusaders returned home. Some stayed and formed a group of four states (the Latin States) on the eastern shore of the Mediterranean.

The Second Crusade (1147–1149) took place because not enough crusaders from the First Crusade stayed to defend the land they had taken. Less than 50 years later, the Turks took back one of the crusaders' four states. A Second Crusade was formed. King Louis VII of France led one army, and Emperor Conrad of Germany led another. But the armies did not work together, and they were defeated.

The Third Crusade (1189–1192) started because the Muslims recaptured the city of Jerusalem in 1187. They also recaptured most of the Holy Land. Saladin was the Muslim leader. Several Europeans led the Third Crusade. But one of them, German Emperor Frederick I, also known as Frederick Barbarossa, died on his way to the Holy Land. Another, King Philip II of France, returned home soon after he arrived. This left King Richard I of England, called "the Lion-Hearted," to fight Saladin's army. Richard defeated Saladin in several battles, but he did not recapture Jerusalem. However, he did succeed in getting Saladin to allow Christians to visit the city on holy pilgrimages.

The Fourth Crusade (1202–1204) was not against the Muslims. Instead, it was an attempt to gain riches and trade. Merchants of Venice, Italy, made a bargain with French nobles. The Venetians supplied the ships to take the French to the Holy Land. The crusaders and the Venetians then got together and captured Constantinople. They removed the Byzantine emperor from his throne. Then they divided up the empire, thus starting its final decline.

The Children's Crusade (1212) was a bizarre episode in the crusades. It was made up of two armies of boys and girls, one from France, the other from Germany. These "soldiers" believed that only children could win the Holy Land for Christianity. Tragically, most of these 50,000 children never reached the Holy Land.

There were four other crusades. None had much success. The failure of the Children's Crusade encouraged Pope Innocent III to begin *The Fifth Crusade* (1217–1221). This managed to capture a town at the mouth of the Nile River, but it was soon given back to the Muslims. *The Sixth Crusade* (1228–1229) was led by Emperor Frederick II of the Holy Roman Empire. He got the Muslims to turn over Jerusalem to the Christians without any fighting, but the Muslims took the city back again in 1244. King Louis IX of France led *The Seventh Crusade* (1248–1254). He was captured, then freed for a huge ransom. Louis sought revenge against the Muslims on *The Eighth Crusade* (1270), but he was old and sick. He died on the way to the Holy Land.

The Crusades brought greater contact between Europe and the Middle East. Trade increased and Europeans

▲ The crusading English King, Richard I, from a 13th-century tile.

▼ To attack the fortified cities and castles of the Muslims, the crusaders used battering rams and tall wooden towers. From the towers they could fire arrows and climb over the walls.

▼ **Lobsters and crabs are one type of crustacean. They live near the ocean shore and are a popular seafood. The American lobster, found in the North Atlantic, has the best meat.**

Mud fiddler crab

Eastern crayfish

learned new skills, such as how to build better ships and draw accurate maps. However, the Crusades did not have as great an influence on Western Europe as historians once believed.

▶ ▶ ▶ ▶ **FIND OUT MORE** ◀ ◀ ◀ ◀
Byzantine Empire; Holy Roman Empire; Palestine

CRUSTACEAN

If you mention the word *crustacean* to someone who likes seafood, he or she will probably think of lobsters, shrimps, or crabs. But these edible and important crustaceans are only a few of the world's 35,000 different kinds. Sandhoppers, woodlice, waterfleas, and barnacles are also crustaceans. Tiny crustaceans of many kinds are such an important source of food for fish and other water animals that much of the life of oceans, lakes, and streams would perish without them.

Crustaceans are *arthropods* of the class *Crustacea*. Insects are

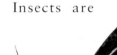

American lobster

Blue crab

arthropods, too, and insects and crustaceans share some features. Like insects and other arthropods, crustaceans have jointed legs, bodies divided into sections or *segments*, and a tough outer covering, or shell, made of a material called *chitin*. Some crustaceans, such as lobsters, have very hard shells, while the shells of other crustaceans are fragile.

Every crustacean hatches from an egg as a larva, which develops into a tiny adult. The adult grows until its shell is too tight, sheds it, and grows a larger one. This process, called *molting*, happens several times before the animal is full grown.

It takes an expert scientist to recognize some crustaceans. Many can be clearly seen only under a microscope. The larvae do not look at all like typical crustaceans.

Crustaceans live in many different places, in both salt and fresh water. Small ones live under the ice in Arctic water. Others survive heat up to 112°F (44°C) in hot springs. Tiny varieties even live in pockets of water caught in leaves of trees. Some live on land but by far the greatest number live in the seas.

The Ten-Legged Crustaceans

The larger crustaceans are called *decapods*, meaning "ten-legged." True *lobsters*, the popular seafood, have four pairs of walking legs. The fifth (front) pair of legs is used for crushing prey and tearing it apart. Most lobsters come from the north Atlantic Ocean, and Maine is especially famous for the lobsters caught off its coast. *Rock lobsters*, also called "spiny lobsters" or "langoustes," belong to a different

LEARN BY DOING

You can easily study the life history of some crustaceans. Brine shrimp can be raised in an aquarium. Buy the shrimp in a pet store and get instructions on how to raise them. Or keep land-living crustaceans, such as "sow bugs" and "pill bugs"—which are not insects—in a terrarium. Feed them a dead caterpillar or earthworm once in a while.

family. They have no pincers. Many of these are caught for food off the coasts of Florida, Africa, and the West Indies. The part we eat, usually called the "tail," is really the animal's abdomen.

Crayfish look like small lobsters, but they do not live in salt water. You can find them under rocks in streams or in mud tunnels on the banks. Crayfish are considered a delicacy in some parts of the United States.

Crabs are much like lobsters, but their tails, or abdomens, do not show. They are neatly tucked away under the animal's shell. Some crabs live in shallow coastal waters. Others are found deep in the ocean. The *rock*, or *cancer*, crab scurries about on land and has legs suited for running. *Blue crabs* are active swimmers, with back legs shaped like small paddles. The largest of all crustaceans is the *spider crab* of Japan, whose outstretched claws may span 11 feet (over 3 m). The *hermit crab* frequently goes "house-hunting." It has no shell of its own on its abdomen. So it "borrows" snail shells or even coconuts as houses, moving to bigger ones as it grows.

Many crabs are good to eat. The blue crab of the Atlantic is caught in enormous numbers by commercial fishermen. Soft-shell crabs, a favorite food, are crabs that have shed their outgrown shells. They are harvested before the new shell hardens. The *Alaska king crab*, also called the *Japanese crab*, is an important food crab, too. These "kings" weigh about 12 pounds (5 kg) apiece. *Horseshoe crabs*, often found washed onto Atlantic beaches, are not really crabs at all, but "living fossils" whose way of life has probably not changed for 175 million years. They are most closely related to spiders and scorpions.

Shrimps and *prawns* are decapods with fragile shells; prawns are a variety of large shrimp. All are good

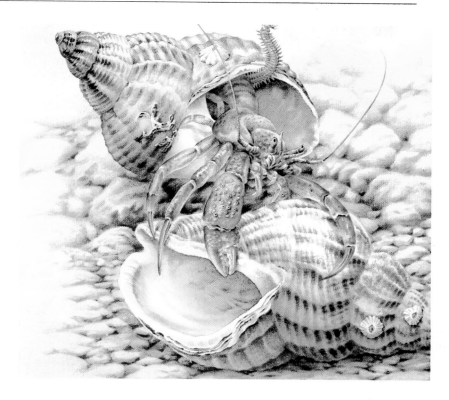

swimmers, equipped with several sets of paddlelike legs. Many kinds of shrimps live in both fresh and salt water. One kind has been found three miles (5 km) deep in the ocean. The ones most often caught for food in the United States belong to the *Pennaeus* genus. They come from the sandy bottom of the Gulf of Mexico. *Mantis shrimp* live in mud burrows and wait for small fish. They slash their prey with hidden jaw blades that act like jackknives.

▲ **The hermit crab is more like a shrimp than a crab. It protects its soft body by living in the old shell of a whelk or other sea snail.**

▼ **Some of the great variety of crustaceans. The common shrimp changes color (from yellow to dark brown) to blend in with its surroundings.**

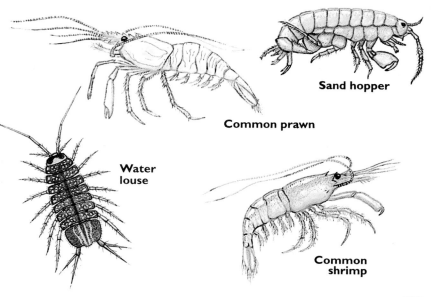

Sand hopper

Common prawn

Water louse

Common shrimp

▲ Barnacles look dead when the tide is out, but open up to feed when it returns. They feed using feathery legs that pick up scraps of food from the water.

Triclinic

Hexagonal

Orthorhombic

Tetragonal

▲ Crystals can be many different shapes. Some are combinations of two or more patterns.

Barnacles

Near the ocean shore, large numbers of *acorn barnacles* sometimes settle on rocks. Each lime-covered shell contains a tiny crustacean. *Gooseneck barnacles* attach themselves to objects such as wharves and ship bottoms. They frequently have to be removed from ships. Other barnacles fasten themselves to sea animals such as whales and turtles.

Barnacles have three distinct stages in their life histories. They hatch from eggs as tiny, free-swimming animals. Then they grow six pairs of legs, two additional eyes, and two large feelers. They later lose their eyes and attach themselves by their heads to solid objects, and a hard shell forms around them. The shell is always made up of five plates of lime-filled material, although barnacle shells come in many shapes. The animals remain in place for all their lives.

The Tiny Crustaceans

The word "zooplankton" is used to describe communities of extremely small, drifting animals in the sea. Often zooplankton communities are so vast they color the water for miles. Crustaceans make up a large part of this moving cloud of sea life. The most abundant of them—and perhaps the most abundant animal in the world—are called *copepods*. They look like shrimp about the size of a rice grain. They swim with jerky movements and feed on algae. Millions of them are eaten by other sea animals. One kind of cold-water, red-colored copepod, known as *krill*, is the main food of herring and baleen whales. Scientists believe that in the future krill will become an important food for humans, too. Krill and other kinds of crustaceans, at sea and in fresh water, are very important to the underwater balance of nature.

▶ ▶ ▶ ▶ **FIND OUT MORE** ◀ ◀ ◀ ◀
Aquarium; Centipedes and Millipedes; Insect; Marine Life; Molting; Shell

☼ CRYOGENICS

You may be familiar with the balloons you can buy that float as if by magic in the air above you. They can do this because they are filled with a gas called *helium*. But if you cool helium to the very low temperature of about -452°F (-269°C) it becomes a liquid. Scientists have discovered that this is a very odd liquid indeed. For example, it is so "runny" that if you were to put it in a cup it would flow up and over the side of the cup! This is called *superfluidity*.

Cryogenics is the study of what happens to things at very low temperatures such as this. Such temperatures are often close to what is called *absolute zero*, the coldest temperature there can possibly be. It is -459.69°F (-273.16°C), although scientists usually describe it as 0K, where "K" stands for "Kelvin." (Kelvins are the same "size" as Celsius degrees, so that 0°C, the freezing point of water, equals 273.16K.)

Some materials behave very oddly at low temperatures. The light gas hydrogen, for example, when cooled almost to absolute zero, becomes a solid that is very like a metal. Many substances display *superconductivity*: if you made a loop out of them and started an electric current in that loop, the electric current would keep flowing around the loop forever!

Some day, scientists hope to achieve superconductivity at room temperature.

▶ ▶ ▶ ▶ **FIND OUT MORE** ◀ ◀ ◀ ◀
Superconductivity

🌐 CRYSTAL

A snowflake, a grain of salt, and a diamond are alike in one way. All are crystals. A *crystal* is a form of matter in which the atoms or molecules are arranged in very regular patterns. Each substance has its own pattern.

The Unit Crystal

Look at some grains of table salt (sodium chloride) with a magnifying glass. Note that each is a tiny cube. (Some may not be cubes because they have been broken, or two or more grains may be stuck together. And other substances, such as iodine, are added to some salt. These other substances do not form cube-shaped crystals.) Each cube is a crystal of salt.

Suppose you had a knife with which you could split a grain of salt as many times as you wished. If you split the grain again and again, you would finally have several million cubes. Each would have edges about one twenty-five-millionth of an inch

Solutions and Crystals

When certain solid substances are put into liquids and moved about, the solid disappears. We say the solid *dissolves* in the liquid. The liquid and the dissolved solid together make up a *solution*. Salt crystals dissolve in water, making a salt solution. When you have dissolved so much solid in a certain amount of a liquid that the liquid can hold no more, you have made a *saturated* solution. Most crystals form in saturated solutions.

▶▶▶▶ **FIND OUT MORE** ◀◀◀◀
Atom; Chemistry; Element; Metal; Mineral

▲ **Some snowflake crystals. The shapes are different depending on the circumstances in which the snowflake formed.**

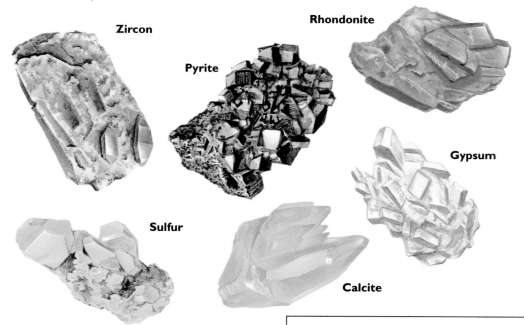

Zircon

Pyrite

Rhondonite

Gypsum

Sulfur

Calcite

◀ **There are six main "systems" (types) of mineral crystal shape. These are based on the size, shape, number, and angle of the faces of each crystal.**

(1 ten-millionth of a centimeter) long. Each cube has 14 chlorine atoms and 13 sodium atoms—one between each pair of chlorine atoms. You cannot split this cube any smaller and still have this arrangement of atoms. That is why this tiny cube is called a *unit crystal*.

The shape of a unit crystal decides the shape of the larger crystal, which is made up of great numbers of unit crystals. Because a unit crystal of sodium chloride is a cube, a grain of salt is also a cube-shaped crystal.

LEARN BY DOING

Find some old jars. Carefully pour some hot water into one of the jars. Take some table salt, sugar, alum (aluminum potassium sulfate) or iron chloride, which you can obtain from drug stores, and stir it into the hot water until no more will dissolve. Pour the mixture into a clean jar and leave it for a while. Crystals will form. Pick out one of the best crystals. Make up some more of the same solution in a clean jar. Attach the crystal to a thread and suspend it from a pencil into the new solution. Watch the crystal as it continues to grow.

CUBA

Capital city
Havana (2,015,000 people)

Area
42,804 square miles (110,861 sq. km)

Population
10,683,000 people

Government
Socialist republic

Natural resources
Sugar, oil, nickel, tobacco

Export products
Sugar, nickel, cigars

Unit of money
Peso

Official language
Spanish

CUBA

Cuba is an island nation in the West Indies, lying about 90 miles (145 km) south of Key West, Florida. It consists of one large island, Cuba, and many smaller ones. Its coastline is fringed with beautiful sandy beaches, coral reefs, and *cays* (low islands). Cuba is almost the same size as Pennsylvania. Cubans call their country the "Pearl of the Antilles" because of its West Indian island beauty. (See the map with the article on WEST INDIES.)

Southeast Cuba has rolling hills, but much of the island consists of lush, flat plains. The climate is warm and sunny all year round, and very dry in some seasons. The temperature often reaches 75°F (24°C) even in the middle of winter.

Sugarcane growing is the biggest industry, and even city workers help during sugarcane harvest. Coffee, rice, beans, and tobacco are also important crops. Cigars made in Havana, Cuba's capital, are famous.

The majority of Cubans are white and of Spanish (or European) descent. Others are black with African ancestry and *mulattos* (persons of mixed black and white ancestry). Cuba also has some persons of Asian descent.

Native tribes lived in Cuba long before the white man came. But they died during the 1500s from overwork as Spanish slaves and from diseases the Europeans brought with them.

Almost all Cubans speak Spanish. Some English is also spoken, however, especially in the large cities, such as Havana and Santiago de Cuba. A few blacks speak a West African language called *Yoruba*.

Columbus discovered Cuba on his first trip to the Americas, in 1492. A Spanish colony was firmly established by 1511. During the next 200 years, Cuba became a center for illegal trade with pirates. England controlled the island for a short time, and then traded it back to Spain for Florida. Cubans grew wealthy from sugar and the slave trade. In time, Spanish rule became unpopular, and political unrest disturbed the island. After the Spanish-American War of 1898, Cuba was freed from Spanish control, but the United States military ruled the country until 1902, when the island became independent.

Fidel Castro led a revolution in the 1950s. Cubans had lost faith in Fulgencio Batista, the dictator who ruled Cuba at that time. Batista fled the country in 1959, and Castro took power. After several disagreements between the U.S. and Cuba, diplomatic relations were ended in 1961. In April of that year, a group of anti-Castro Cubans supported by the U.S.

© 1994 GeoSystems, an R.R. Donnelley & Sons Company

landed at a place called the Bay of Pigs to try to overthrow Castro. But the attack was poorly planned, and Castro's army was well organized. He quickly defeated them.

Cuba became a Communist state under Castro, who turned to the then Soviet Union for military and economic aid. The Soviets built missile bases on the island. On October 22, 1962, President Kennedy demanded that the Soviets remove all missiles or risk war with the United States. He also ordered a naval blockade of Cuba. Soviet Premier Nikita Khrushchev agreed to remove the missiles, and Kennedy lifted the blockade.

Castro has resisted the social and economic reforms that have taken place in the Soviet Union. Cuban troops have been withdrawn from aiding revolutionary groups in Africa. Cuba is now facing economic difficulties with the end of Soviet aid.

▶▶▶▶ FIND OUT MORE ◀◀◀◀
Castro, Fidel; Kennedy, John Fitzgerald; Spanish-American War; West Indies

CULTURE

If you tried to eat your dinner by kneeling at the table instead of sitting in a chair, and if you dug your fork into the bowls of food at the center of the table instead of putting a portion of food on your plate, your parents would probably tell you that you were being very rude. But you could do these things—and eat with chopsticks instead of a knife, fork, and spoon—if you lived in Japan. You would have good table manners, according to Japanese culture.

Culture is how a particular group of people behave. From earliest times, people have lived together in groups. A group might be very small, a few families living together in a village. Or it might be as large as a whole nation. The group develops a language, a government, laws, religious beliefs, and a particular type of art. The word *culture* means all these things together.

A cultured person is one who has learned the way of life of his or her culture. The way we speak, our manners, our ideas of good art and good literature, the songs we sing, the clothes we wear, even the games we play are all parts of our culture.

Cultures change all the time. So do their languages. Everyone now knows what a microcomputer is— you may even have one of your own—but only a few years ago the word did not exist. Ideas about dress change, too. Ask your parents or

▲ Havana, the capital city of Cuba, is famous for its cigars.

▼ Although Western culture is mainly based on the ancient civilizations of Greece and Rome, their lives were often quite different from ours. For example, the Romans liked to eat reclining on couches around a low table.

your teacher what students wore to school 20 years ago. Does it sound as though clothing was the same then as now?

People "belong" to more than one culture. A large culture is made up of several smaller ones. The United States is part of *Western culture,* the culture based mostly on ancient

▲ Punishment in the English colonies of America during the 17th century was usually inflicted in public in order to bring disgrace upon the offender.

Greece and Rome that developed in Europe. Judeo-Christian religious beliefs have become an important part of Western culture.

People in the United States also belong to North American culture. And even this is made up of other cultures. If you live on a farm in the Midwest, you have many different habits from a person who lives in a large Eastern city. But in some ways cultures are becoming more and more alike. For example, in almost every capital city in the world you can now see the same makes of automobile and the same restaurant chains. This can lead to *assimilation* where one group's culture is over-

▼ These firewalkers in Hong Kong feel little or no pain as they tread on the red-hot coals. Firewalking is one small part of their Eastern culture.

whelmed by another's and theirs disappears. This nearly happened to Native American culture.

The culture of a group is passed on to its children. But one culture can "borrow" from another. Although Western culture came mainly from the ancient civilizations of Greece and Rome, parts of other cultures were borrowed, too. If you enjoy country music, you may think the banjo is a North American instrument. But it is an instrument borrowed from African culture. In the same way, pieces of the cultures of China, Japan, and other countries have become part of our culture. However, some parts of U.S. culture are original to it. The automobile and the airplane were not borrowed from another culture. This is called "invented" culture.

▶ ▶ ▶ ▶ **FIND OUT MORE** ◀ ◀ ◀ ◀
Anthropology; Civilization; Customs; Sociology

CURIE FAMILY

Marie and her husband Pierre Curie are famous for their work on radioactivity. Their daughters Irène and Eve, and their son-in-law Frédéric, also became well known.

Marie Sklodowska Curie (1867-1934) was born in Warsaw, Poland. She traveled to Paris, France, to study chemistry and physics. There she met Pierre Curie (1859-1906), a brilliant French scientist. Marie and Pierre were married in 1895.

The next year, a French scientist named Antoine Henri Becquerel discovered the radioactivity of uranium ore, or *pitchblende.* Marie and Pierre began to experiment with radioactivity even though they had little money for research. They soon realized the ore was more radioactive than pure uranium, so they guessed that another material must be causing the "extra" radioactivity. They set out to find this material, and they discovered two new radioactive elements—*polonium* and *radium*. Marie and Pierre were able to extract tiny amounts of these elements from several tons of pitchblende by working hard and long.

The Curies, together with Becquerel, shared the Nobel Prize for physics in 1903. Marie was the first woman to receive this award. She received a second one for chemistry in 1911—the first person ever to win two Nobel prizes.

Irène Joliot-Curie (1897–1956) was her mother's assistant in the Radiation Institute in Paris and the third member of the Curie family to win a Nobel Prize. She and her husband, Jean Frédéric Joliot-Curie (1900–1958; original surname Joliot), made discoveries that helped later scientists produce radioactive forms of elements that are not normally radioactive. The Joliot-Curies won the Nobel Prize for chemistry in 1935. Like Marie, the Joliot-Curies both died of cancer, probably because of the radioactivity with which they all worked. (Pierre was killed in a street accident.) Eve Curie (born 1904) is a musician and author. Her most famous book is *Madam Curie*, a biography of her mother.

▶▶▶▶ **FIND OUT MORE** ◀◀◀◀
Element; Radioactivity

CURLING

The team game of curling probably began in Scotland or Holland in the early 1500s. The game is similar to bowling but is played with granite stones on frozen lakes or indoor ice rinks. Curling is popular today in Canada, Scandinavia, and in some parts of the United States.

Curling players slide heavy, rounded stones, with metal handles attached, on an ice court toward a round target. The ice court is 146 feet (44.5 m) long and 14 feet (4.25 m) wide. The object of the game is to slide the stones as close as possible to the center of a target, a three-ringed bull's-eye on the ice. The target's center is called the *tee* or *button*. Two four-person teams, called *rinks*, compete in a curling match. The rink that gets the greatest number of stones nearest the tee wins.

The rink or team captain, called the *skip*, tells his or her rinkmates where and how hard to slide their stones. Each rink has eight stones. Each player uses two of these, as he or she takes turns curling against a player from the

▲ Players are allowed to sweep away frost and water from in front of a stone to make it move faster along the ice.

opposing rink. When all the stones of both rinks have been played, this is called an *end* (inning), and scores are totaled. Ten ends usually make a game.

Curling stones are made of real stone. Each stone usually weighs 38 pounds (17 kg), but they can weigh as little as 35 (16 kg) or as much as 50 (23 kg). The stone is about 36 inches (90 cm) around. The top and bottom of the stone are flat and slightly scooped out. A handle is attached

▲ Marie and Pierre Curie, with their daughter Irène.

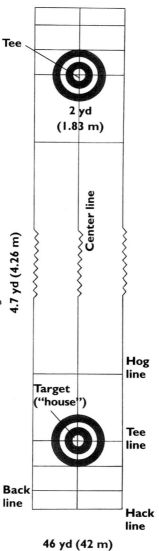

Tee

2 yd
(1.83 m)

Center line

4.7 yd (4.26 m)

Hog line

Target ("house")

Tee line

Back line

Hack line

46 yd (42 m)

▲ The playing area in curling.

▲ A curling stone is shaped from granite with a steel band around the middle. The base is polished to reduce friction.

▲ George Armstrong Custer was only 24 when he was promoted, briefly, to the rank of brigadier general during the Civil War.

through a hole that is drilled through the stone from top to bottom.

To slide a stone, a player holds it by its handle and tries to give it a slight twist as he or she slides it forward. The twist makes the stone spin, or *curl*, as it slides, which gives the game its name. Each rink tries to aim its stones to knock its opponents' stones out of the target boundaries. The players all carry brooms with them to sweep frost from the ice ahead of a rinkmate's sliding stone.

▶▶▶▶ **FIND OUT MORE** ◀◀◀◀
Bowling; Games; Sports

CURRENT

SEE OCEAN

CUSTER, GEORGE (1839–1876)

George Armstrong Custer was an army officer and Indian fighter. Historians do not agree whether the decision he made to attack at the battle of the Little Big Horn was right or not.

Custer was born in New Rumley, Ohio. He dreamed of becoming a soldier and graduated from West Point in 1861. In the Civil War he fought as a cavalry officer at Bull Run, Gettysburg, and Richmond. During the war he became the youngest general in the Union Army.

Settlers swarmed westward after the war, killing the buffalo and driving the Plains tribes from their homes. The Native Americans fought back. The army began to force them onto reservations. Custer, who held the rank of lieutenant colonel, commanded the famous Seventh Cavalry in many brutal attacks on the Sioux and Cheyenne tribes.

In 1876, he led a column of soldiers in search of Sioux who had left their Black Hills reservation to hunt buffalo. He found them at the Little Big Horn River in Montana. He was supposed to wait for reinforcements, but he attacked on June 25, before other troops could arrive. About 2,500 braves, led by chiefs Sitting Bull and Crazy Horse, surrounded "Yellow Hair," as the Native Americans called him, and his soldiers. Custer and all his men were killed.

There were arguments after the defeat. Some thought Custer was a vain fool who disobeyed orders. Others honored his memory. The argument may never be settled.

▶▶▶▶ **FIND OUT MORE** ◀◀◀◀
Indian Wars; Native Americans

▶ Custer and all of his 265 soldiers were killed at the Battle of the Little Big Horn. It came to be known as "Custer's Last Stand."

CUSTOMS

Why do many people shake hands when they meet? Why do Japanese bow to each other in greeting? They are following customs. Customs are ways of acting and living—learned and followed by a great many people—that have come down from generation to generation. Customs often change as time goes by and the lives of people change.

How does a custom start? Many develop because people find them the easiest, most convenient way to do things. For example, it is a custom to close schools during the summer. This practice was begun so that children could help with the harvest. Some customs begin because some people believe certain ways of behaving are proper and good. Other customs come from religious beliefs.

Some are taken more seriously than others. Some have become laws of the land. These are sometimes called mores, the Latin word for "customs." Many written laws have come from mores, and persons who break these laws are punished. For example, people in most countries drive their cars on the right-hand side of the road. They can be arrested, or have accidents, if they drive on the left side. In some African tribes and in several Muslim countries, it is considered proper for a man to have more than one wife at a time, but this practice of polygamy is against the law in the United States.

Some customs are short-lived and can really be called *fashions*. Such fashions may include ways of dressing, length of hair (short or long), and beards. Fashions can become customs through long use. Shaking hands when you meet someone may have begun in the early Middle Ages. When one knight met another, they would shake hands to prove they were not carrying hidden weapons.

People even practice a few customs that were originally *superstitions*. Superstitions are unscientific beliefs that certain actions will cause good luck, happiness, bad luck, death, pain, or other events. For example, you have probably been told it is rude to point at people. Long ago people believed pointing at someone was a way of killing that person by magic.

▲ **It is the custom in many countries to celebrate the new year. The Chinese New Year begins in late January or early February and is celebrated in Chinese communities around the world.**

▲ **On Halloween many people carve jack-o'-lanterns out of pumpkins. Halloween probably came from ancient new year festivals and festivals of the dead.**

▶▶▶▶ **FIND OUT MORE** ◀◀◀◀
Burial Customs; Clothing; Culture; Fashion; Habit; Hairstyle; Manners

CYBERNETICS

SEE COMPUTER

CYCLONE

SEE WEATHER

◀ **When a Jewish boy turns 13, the event is celebrated with a bar mitzvah. The boy reads from the Torah, the Jewish Law. After this he takes on the religious duties of an adult.**

CYPRUS

Capital city
Nicosia (167,000 people)

Area
3,572 square miles
(9,251 sq. km)

Population
742,000 people

Government
Constitutional republic

Natural resources
Marble, clay, asbestos, chromite, iron pyrites, copper

Export products
Grapes, citrus fruits, potatoes, wine, clothing, shoes

Unit of money
Pound

Official languages
Greek, Turkish

▼ **A fortified castle built in the 12th century near Limassol, on the island of Cyprus.**

738

CYPRUS

The rocky coast of Cyprus rises out of the eastern Mediterranean. (See the map with the article on EUROPE.) Parts of the island are covered by cedar forests. Two mountain chains cross Cyprus from east to west. Between them lies a fertile plain. Small villages dot the countryside, surrounded by wheat fields and groves of oranges and lemons. Farmers also grow bananas, grapes, and olives.

Most Cypriots are of Greek or Turkish origin. Cyprus was ruled by Egypt, Greece, and the Roman Empire at different times during its early history. A legend tells that Greek heroes founded settlements on the island of Cyprus 5,000 years ago. The Turks conquered the island in the 1500s. They ruled there for 300 years. Cyprus came under British rule in 1878. Britain gave the island independence in 1960.

The Cypriots then raised the white flag—a symbol of peace—of their new republic. But an old quarrel divides the 550,000 Greek Cypriots from the 150,000 Turkish Cypriots. Greek Cypriots believe that the Turks are intruders. Many want Cyprus to be united with Greece.

Since 1964, serious fighting has erupted between the Turkish and Greek Cypriots. The United Nations has sent various peacekeeping forces to work out a solution and to establish a unified government. Archbishop Makarios tried unsuccessfully as President to end the fighting until his death in 1977. In 1975, the Turks set up their own government in the north. In 1983 the Turkish Cypriots declared the Turkish Republic of Northern Cyprus an independent nation, but it has yet to be internationally recognized.

▶▶▶▶ **FIND OUT MORE** ◀◀◀◀
Greece; Mediterranean Sea; Turkey

CZAR

SEE RUSSIAN HISTORY

CZECH REPUBLIC

The Czech Republic is a country in central Europe. Until 1993 it was part of a larger country, Czechoslovakia, which was ruled by Communists until 1989. The other part of Czechoslovakia, Slovakia, is also independent.

The Czech Republic is bordered by

Poland on the north, Slovakia on the east, Austria on the south, and Germany on the west and northwest. The Republic itself is made up of two regions. *Bohemia* in the west, is a land of hilly forests. Prague, the capital, is located there. To the east is *Moravia,* where there are large farms on the wide and rolling plains.

Most of the industries of the Czech Republic are located in Bohemia. Manufacturing is important, and factories produce steel, glass, automobiles, beer, and ammu-

communism became known as the "Velvet Revolution" because there was little violence. Vaclav Havel, a playwright and human rights campaigner, was elected president.

Slovak leaders began to demand more independence. In 1992, the Czechs and the Slovaks agreed to divide Czechoslovakia into two independent countries. This split, known as the "Velvet Divorce," became effective on January 1, 1993.

nition. Others process oil and chemical goods. Moravian farms produce wheat, sugar beets, potatoes, rye, and barley.

The Republic takes its name from the Czechs, a Slavic people who lived in Bohemia and Moravia. The king of Bohemia made Prague one of the great European cities in the 1300s. Many cities in the Czech Republic date back to that era. Later, Bohemia and Moravia became part of the Austrian Empire. Austrian rule ended in 1918, at which time Bohemia and Moravia joined neighboring Slovakia to form Czechoslovakia.

Germany controlled Czechoslovakia during World War II and the Soviet Union dominated the country after the war. Soviet troops crushed Czech efforts to develop a freer type of communism in 1968.

Czechoslovakia broke free of Communist rule in 1989. The fall of

Map labels: Decin, Liberec, Snezka 5,256 ft. 1,602 m., Teplice, Usti nad Labem, Krkonose Mts., Most, Chomutov, Karlovy Vary, Kladno, Elbe R., Hradec Kralove, Jesenik Mts., Prague, Berounka R., Pardubice, Morava R., Opava, Ostrava, Karvina, Havirov, Frydek-Mistek, Plzen, Vltava, Sazava R., Oder R., Olomouc, Prostejov, Prerov, BOHEMIAN FOREST Sumava Mts., Jihlava, Zlin, Ceske Budejovice, Brno, Dyje R.

0   50   100 Miles
0   50   100   150 Kilometers
© 1994 GeoSystems, an R.R. Donnelley & Sons Company

▶ ▶ ▶ ▶ **FIND OUT MORE** ◀ ◀ ◀ ◀
Europe; Slovakia

◀ **The Defenestration of Prague in 1618. Officials of the Holy Roman Emperor were thrown out of a window in Prague castle, starting the Thirty Years War.**

St. Wenceslas was a prince who lived in the city of Prague in the 900s. He is known as the patron saint of Bohemia, now part of the Czech Republic.

DEVELOPMENT OF THE LETTER D

d	The Semitic D c. 1500 BC
◁	The Phoenician D c. 1000 BC
△	The Greek D c. 600 BC
D	The Roman D c. AD 600

DADAISM

In 1914, World War I broke out. Many artists had already been disgusted by the society they lived in and its lack of interest in new forms of art. Now they had to join the armies of their countries, whether they liked it or not. In 1915, a few artists met and decided to start a series of "anti-art" activities in order to ridicule art and confuse art lovers rather than to create art.

The name they gave to their new movement, Dada, tells us how their minds worked. They stabbed at a dictionary with a penknife and hit the word *dada*, the French for "hobbyhorse." They used it because they liked its sound and nonsense meaning.

The public was indeed confused. One Dadaist, Kurt Schwitters, made compositions out of rubbish. The public was invited to a show of Dadaist "art" where visitors were given hatchets and invited to destroy an exhibit. The Dadaists gave absurd lectures and entertainments, such as a dance where the performers were dressed in stovepipes. The public was outraged which greatly pleased the Dadaists.

Though Dadaism was mainly European, there were some Dadaists in the United States too. Modern art was unpopular in the United States, but Alfred Stieglitz, a New York photographer, ran a gallery where it was shown. Dadaists, including some Europeans, gathered there.

Out of the apparent madness of Dada came some valuable artistic techniques. Germans invented photographic collage, in which bits of photographs are glued together to give a vivid impression of something, such as a city. Dada publications used type in new and daring ways. Dada's use of machine forms—symbolizing modern life—anticipated the

▲ The spirit of Dada is still seen in modern art. This is *Dalmatian Lamp*, a work of 1972 by the U.S. artist Karen Breschi.

use of advertising art, comic-strip drawing, and other familiar things used by the Pop artists in the 1960s.

In 1918, a Dada political movement began in Germany to denounce the military authorities. The war ended in November 1918, though, and the Dadaists returned to the creation of art. After 1922, what was left of Dadaism was absorbed by Surrealism.

▶▶▶ **FIND OUT MORE** ◀◀◀
Surrealism

DAEDALUS

One of the ancient Greek myths is about a famed builder, inventor, and sculptor named Daedalus.

One of his students, his nephew Talos, was so brilliant that Daedalus became jealous and killed him. Daedalus fled from Athens to the island of Crete. King Minos, ruler of Crete, asked Daedalus to build the *Labyrinth* (a winding maze of passageways) to imprison the Minotaur, a horrible monster who was half man and half bull.

King Minos later became angry at Daedalus and imprisoned him and his son Icarus in the Labyrinth. To escape, Daedalus made wings from feathers and wax for himself and Icarus. They flew from Crete but

◀ Icarus, the son of Daedalus, escaping on man-made wings. But Icarus flew too near the sun, which melted his wings, and he plunged to his death.

Icarus foolishly flew too near the sun. His wings melted and he fell into the sea (now called the Icarian Sea) and drowned. Daedalus finally landed safely on the island of Sicily, where he waited in vain for his son.

▶▶▶▶ **FIND OUT MORE** ◀◀◀◀
Maze; Mythology

DAIRY FARMING

The industry that processes and sells products such as milk, cheese, and butter is called dairying. The animals that produce milk are raised and tended on dairy farms. In some countries goats, sheep, reindeer, camels, or water buffalo are the milk producers. But much of our milk comes from cows.

Modern dairy farms vary enormously in size. Some have almost 1,000 cows, but most average about 40. An average farm may have about 200 acres (800 sq. km) of land. Some of the land is needed for growing hay, corn, soybeans, and other plants for making cattle-feed. The cows must also have spacious pastures where they can graze and exercise. A dairy farm usually has a large, two-story barn. The ground floor has stalls where the cows are milked and where they are sheltered during the cold months. The second floor has lofts piled with hay and bins full of grain. A silo, a tall, windowless tower is used to store cattle-feed made of chopped cornstalks and other grasses. This feed is saved for the wintertime, when the cows have no grass to eat.

Milking the Cows
A cow's body begins to produce milk a short time before the birth of a calf. The calf normally feeds on its mother's milk for several months after birth. When it is old enough to eat solid food, its mother stops giving milk. In order to milk the cow, the dairy farmer must take the calf from its mother after only a few days. The farmer teaches the calf to drink milk from a pail, using a rubber nipple. A regularly milked cow will then keep producing milk for many years.

Most cows are milked at least twice a day. If they are not milked regularly, their *udders* (milk glands) become painful. Special milking machines are used. The machine fits onto the four *teats* (nipples) of the cow's udder. Four suction cups draw out the milk.

Many large dairy farms have a special room called a *milking parlor,* which has stalls on a raised platform. The cow walks up a ramp and into one of the stalls. Feed is automatically placed in the trough before her,

▲ More than 17 billion gallons (64 billion liters) of milk are produced in the United States each year. There are strict laws governing its production and distribution.

▲ **Cows are milked quickly and efficiently by machines in the milking parlor.**

More people in the world drink goat's milk than cow's milk.

▼ **Cheese, a dairy product, on display in a shop in France. France is the third largest cheese producer.**

and the milking machine is attached to her teats. As she munches her food, the machine milks her and pumps the milk into a central tank. When the milking is finished, the stall is unlocked and the cow walks out.

Milk can spoil easily, so it must be refrigerated as soon as it comes from the cow. Most dairy farms deliver milk daily to a dairy plant for processing and distributing. The milk can be carried long distances without spoiling in a refrigerated truck or railroad car.

▶▶▶▶ **FIND OUT MORE** ◀◀◀◀
Cattle; Dairy Products

DAIRY PRODUCTS

Milk is one of our most important foods. It is the basic product of the dairy industry and the raw material used to make all other dairy products. Milk is the liquid produced by all female mammals to feed their young. Cow's milk is the main kind of milk drunk in the United States.

Milk is an excellent food. For most people, it is easy to digest, although some cannot. Those who cannot digest milk have a *lactose intolerance*. Milk tastes good, and has many nutrients important to growth. Milk is made of water, proteins, fats, sugars, and various minerals. It contains vitamin A, vitamin B_2 (riboflavin), and calcium, a mineral important to the growth and health of bone.

Making dairy products is a big and complicated business. The milk you drink goes through many processes in the complex machines of the modern dairy plant before you buy it at the supermarket. Milk is *pasteurized*, heated to kill harmful bacteria. Most milk is *homogenized*, that is, fat particles are made much smaller and dispersed through the rest of the milk.

When milk is not homogenized, fat quickly rises to the top, where it forms cream, which is used for fine baking and flavoring. Butter results when milk or cream is *churned* (stirred rapidly). When cream is removed from unhomogenized milk, skim milk is left. Skim milk contains all of milk's nutrients except vitamin A, which is in the cream. Skim milk has less fat than whole milk, so it is good for people who are trying to lose weight or who have heart ailments.

Concentrated milk products include evaporated milk, condensed milk, and dried (powdered) milk. All are made by heating pasteurized milk to remove water from it. About half the water is removed to make evaporated milk, which is almost always canned. Condensed milk is made the same way, but sugar is added first.

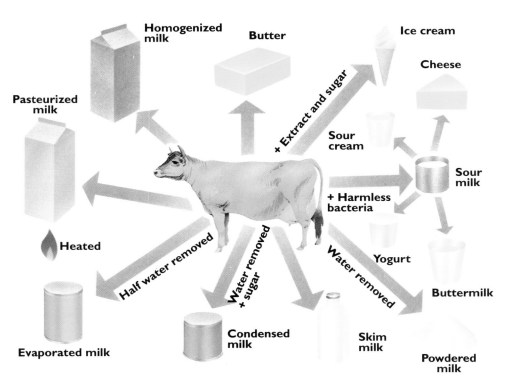

Homogenized milk

Butter

Ice cream

Cheese

Pasteurized milk

+ Extract and sugar

Sour cream

Sour milk

+ Harmless bacteria

Heated

Half water removed

Water removed + sugar

Water removed

Yogurt

Buttermilk

Evaporated milk

Condensed milk

Skim milk

Powdered milk

◀ This diagram illustrates the many different kinds of dairy products that come from a cow.

Condensed milk keeps a very long time because the sugar prevents bacteria from turning the milk sour. Almost all the water is removed to make dried milk. It is as nourishing as fresh milk when the water is replaced. Dried milk can also be kept a very long time without spoiling. It is light in weight and compact, so it can easily be shipped over long distances.

Several other products are made when other substances are added to milk or cream. Different types of harmless acid-producing bacteria are added to turn milk sour. Sour milk is used to make cheese, sour cream, yogurt, and buttermilk. When sugar and some other ingredients, such as egg whites or gelatin, are mixed with cream, milkfat, or butterfat and the mixture is frozen, the result is ice cream or sherbet.

▶ ▶ ▶ ▶ **FIND OUT MORE** ◀ ◀ ◀ ◀
Cattle; Cheese; Dairy Farming; Ice Cream; Nutrition; Pasteur, Louis

DAKOTAS

SEE SIOUX

DALI, SALVADOR

SEE SURREALISM

DALLAS

With over a million people, Dallas, Texas, is the eighth largest city in the United States. It is nicknamed "Big D." It is a major business, financial, and industrial center, producing such things as electronics and electrical equipment and parts for aircraft and missiles. Dallas is also famed for its fashion industry. Its many educational institutions include the Southern Methodist University, which opened in 1915.

Dallas was founded in 1841 by a trader, John Neely Bryan, who built a cabin on the Trinity River. People argue about the origin of the city's name. Some believe that it was named for one of Bryan's friends. Others think that it was named for a U.S. Vice President, George Mifflin Dallas (1792–1864). The city grew rapidly after the arrival of railroads in the early 1870s. Dallas became the country's most important cotton

▼ **Dallas, in Texas, is one of the richest cities in the United States.**

743

▲ A buttress dam. The buttresses support the dam against the force of the water.

LARGEST DAMS IN THE U.S. (by volume)

1. **New Cornelia Tailings, Ten Mile Wash, Arizona**
2. **Fort Peck, Missouri River, Montana**
3. **Oahe Tailings, Missouri River, South Dakota**
4. **Orovill, Feather River, California**
5. **San Luis, San Luis River, California**
6. **Garrison, Missouri River, North Dakota**

▼ The Hoover Dam on the Colorado River. The dam is a gravity-arch dam. Inset is a diagram of its layout.

market. Industries developed and Dallas has stayed in the forefront of industrial technology ever since.

State Fair Park, site of the Texas State Fair every October, attracts tourists with its museums and Cotton Bowl football stadium. Other attractions include the famous and expensive Neiman-Marcus store and the Reunion Tower, which offers fine views of Dallas. But the city's most photographed building is the Texas Book Depository, from which President John F. Kennedy was shot on November 22, 1963. Nearby stands the John F. Kennedy Memorial, 30 feet (9 m) high.

▶▶▶▶ **FIND OUT MORE** ◀◀◀◀
Texas

DAM

A dam is a structure built to hold back the water of a river or stream. A dam may block the flow of a river so that the water is stored for irrigating crops in dry seasons. The stored water may be used to produce electricity (*hydro-electricity*). A dam built on a shallow river often makes the water behind the dam deep enough for large ships to sail on it. Part of the Panama Canal was formed by damming the Chagres River to make Gatun Lake, which is deep enough for oceangoing vessels to steam across. Other dams are built mainly to control flooding.

More than 40 dams have been built in the valley of the Tennessee River. The dams are built and operated by the Tennessee Valley Authority (TVA), a U.S. government agency. The dams provide flood control, electric power, navigable waters, and lakes for swimming, fishing, and boating by holding back water or channeling it in certain directions.

Kinds of Dams

Concrete, stone, and earth are most often used to make dams.

The *gravity dam*—usually built of rock or concrete—is wider at the bottom than at the top. A gravity dam's shape and great weight keep it in place against the tremendous pushing force of the water that it holds back. Some gravity dams are solid. Others are hollow and are reinforced by walls called buttresses.

Diversion tunnels

Single-arch dams are usually constructed in narrow gorges or canyons. The arch curves so that the sides are farther downstream than the center. This arrangement transfers the force of the water to the side of the canyon. Wider rivers may be blocked by a *multiple-arch dam.* Thick, solid concrete towers between arches give the dam strength. Gravity and arch dams are built of either concrete or masonry (large stones held together by mortar). The stones may be cut to fit together like bricks.

Earth-fill dams are made of a mixture of sand, clay, and silt. Water can seep through an earth dam, so most have a waterproof inner section of steel or concrete that runs the whole length of the dam. In small earth-fill dams the inner section may be soft. The earth piled on either side of the inner section gives it strength. The upstream side of an earth dam is usually covered by a thick coating of waterproof material.

Spillways and Gates

Although built to block a river, a dam must allow water to pass downstream. This is done by means of spillways and gates.

A *spillway* is a section of the top of the dam that is lower than the rest. When the stored water rises close to the top of the dam, it flows over the spillway and downstream.

Instead of a spillway, a dam may have one or more *gates* that can be opened and closed by machinery. Water flows downstream through the open gates. The gates can be closed when rain is heavy, so the land downstream is not flooded. The extra water can be allowed to flow slowly downstream after the rain is over.

When certain rivers are dammed up, some migratory fish, like the salmon, cannot reach their spawning grounds. To help such fish breed, *fish ladders* are built beside the dams which fish can swim up.

About 3,000 large dams have been built in the United States. Remains of dams more than 6,000 years old have been found along the Tigris and Euphrates rivers in Iraq. The ancient Romans built many dams in Europe and Africa, and some are still in use.

▶▶▶▶ **FIND OUT MORE** ◀◀◀◀
Abu Simbel; Flood; Hydroelectricity; Irrigation; Panama Canal; Water Supply

DAMOCLES

Damocles belonged to the court of Dionysius the Elder, ruler of Syracuse, Sicily, in the 300s B.C. Damocles once mistakenly flattered Dionysius, telling him how lucky he was to be wealthy and happy, so the king decided to teach Damocles a lesson. Dionysius invited Damocles to a great feast, where he was given everything he wanted. During the feast, Damocles looked up and saw a sharp sword held by a single hair hanging over his own head. Dionysius was showing Damocles that even a powerful person such as himself cannot always be safe and content. The term *sword of Damocles* means "a disaster to come," or "a threat of disaster."

DANCE

Dance is probably the oldest of the arts. Early people may have shown how they felt by moving their bodies in ways that expressed this feeling. Maybe they jumped, waved their arms, clapped their hands, and stamped their feet. They may have danced to tell a story. They used expressive movements to celebrate the important moments in life. Marriage, birth, death, and the beginning of war all had specific dance patterns. The patterns gradually came to be considered magic. People imitated animals, hoping to be lucky in the hunt. People danced before planting

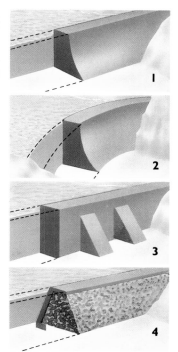

▲ **Four different types of dams. 1. Gravity dams made of concrete or stone take the whole weight of the water.**
2. Arch dams are curved to deflect the immense pressure of the water against the canyon walls.
3. Buttress dams are strengthened.
4. Earth-fill dams are heaps of earth and rock covered with a layer of masonry or concrete.

WHERE TO DISCOVER MORE

Ancona, George. *Dancing Is.* New York: Elsevier-Dutton, 1981.
Gherman, Beverly. *Agnes de Mille: Dancing off the Earth.* New York: Atheneum Publishers, 1990.

▲ Dancing figures have been found in the wall paintings of ancient Egypt.

▲ Morris dancing is a form of English folk dance begun in the Middle Ages.

▲ Ballet dancing grew out of the court dances of the 18th century. At this time they began to be performed in public.

or harvesting to ensure good crops. People danced to arouse emotion and build strength before going into battle. Ritual or religious dance grew from belief in the power of rhythmic motion.

As people developed cities, dance changed. Religious dance was no longer for all the people but was done by men or women connected with a temple. Some of the temple dances of the Hindus in India today are much the same as they were 2,000 years ago. Ancient Egyptian dance is known only through wall paintings. We know little about dance in Biblical times, except that the Bible mentions that people danced. King David danced for joy to celebrate a victory. In ancient Greece, sculpture and pottery paintings show dancers.

As rulers became powerful and wealthy, a kind of dance developed simply for their entertainment. Each land developed different kinds of ceremonial dance. This dancing, neither part of religion nor folk dancing for pleasure, was the beginning of dance as a form of art.

Dance as an Art

Ballet and modern dance are the two main kinds of dance art. *Ballet* dates back several centuries. It grew out of dances done in European courts. Based on traditional rules, ballet uses dancing on the toes and other special movements, and often tells a story. A ballet is done with music, stage settings, and costumes. Ballet sometimes has an important place in the opera.

Modern dance has grown out of traditional ballet. It is a freer kind of movement. Isadora Duncan helped show the way to this new kind of dance by using her body in free expression, moving naturally and gracefully. There is music in modern dance, as in the ballet. It may be made by machines ("electronic")

instead of by traditional musical instruments. Sometimes modern dance tells a story and uses costumes and settings. But modern dances may simply express some idea or emotion, or just exhibit beautiful patterns of movement with no meaning at all.

In recent decades, musical stage shows such as *Oklahoma, West Side Story,* and *Chorus Line* have presented skillful, well-planned dancing that is part of the story. Movies and television, especially MTV, have made much use of this form of the dance art.

Planning Dances

As the writer uses words and the composer combines sounds, so the *choreographer* makes up a dance, whether ballet or modern. Choreographers decide which dance steps will best tell the story, which music to use, and what costumes the dancers will wear. They then teach each new dance to the performers.

Choreographers in the past always kept the patterns of their dances (the *choreography*) in their heads. From time to time, someone has tried to write down dances so they can be repeated later. Two systems of dance notation, or dance writing, are now in use by choreographers. Both use a kind of shorthand.

▼ Gene Kelly, shown here with Anne Miller in the musical *On the Town,* was famous for his athletic style of dance.

Folk Dancing

Although some types of dancing are for art, most people dance for recreation—for fun. In the Middle Ages in Europe, folk dancing was done by the ordinary people, the peasants. They danced for fun at holiday gatherings. Most folk dances were and are done by groups of people. Sometimes folk dances are called *ethnic* (cultural, or racial) dances because different groups or races of people each developed their own dances.

Square dancing is an example of folk dancing. English country dancing, Spanish classical dancing, and Mexican folk dancing are others. Some folk-dance groups, like the Ballet Folklorico of Mexico, have professional dancers.

Citizens of many countries today treasure their traditional dances as signs of national unity. The *hula* dancers of Hawaii, for example, can tell the history of their islands through their movements.

Ballroom Dancing

The noblemen and their ladies in the courts of European countries danced the *minuet*, the *gavotte*, and the *pavan*. In time a new kind of dancing called ballroom dancing evolved from these dances. Many people, both rich and poor, took up ballroom dancing. The *polka* and the *waltz* were two kinds of early ballroom dancing.

Lively, catchy ragtime music became very popular in the late 19th century. Ragtime and other forms of music developed into jazz, and new dances were made up to fit this new music. The *foxtrot* became an important new dance and is still enjoyed today. The *Charleston* was a very fast dance popular in the 1920s. Dances from Africa and from South American countries (such as the *tango*, *rumba*, and *samba*, from Argentina, Brazil, and Cuba) also became popular in the 1930s and 1940s.

Ballroom dancing is done by couples. Partners face each other and perform certain steps together in time to music. Dance steps are usually based on a walking step, but patterns are different for different dances. The basic waltz and foxtrot are two popular ballroom dances.

Rock 'n' Roll Dancing

With the popularity of rock 'n' roll music in the 1950s and 1960s, a dance called *bop* was created. It was based on *jitterbugging*, the fast and energetic dance of the 1940s. Other *fad* dances, such as the *twist*, *monkey*, and *swim* of the rock 'n' roll years and disco in the 1970s, became very popular for only a short time. Today's dancing has no fixed movements, but this may change in times to come. Couples who dance to hard rock music dance more or less independently of each other.

Other Kinds of Dancing

Ice skating or roller skating to dance music, alone or with a partner, is another kind of dancing that is fun. Dance is also an important part of some gymnastic exercises and synchronized swimming.

▶▶▶▶ **FIND OUT MORE** ◀◀◀◀
Composers for Art Dance see Bernstein, Leonard; Copland, Aaron; Mendelssohn, Felix; Stravinsky, Igor; Tchaikovsky, Peter Ilyich
Dancers see Duncan, Isadora; Nijinsky, Vaslav; Pavlova, Anna
Kinds of Dance see Ballet; Folk Dancing; Musical Comedy; Opera; Square Dancing

▲ In ballroom dancing, a couple must move together well, keep in time with the music, and be graceful if they are to succeed.

▲ This African dance dates from the distant past. Many African dances are ceremonial.

DANTE ALIGHIERI (1265–1321)

Dante's *Divine Comedy* is one of the most important and beautiful poems in the world. Dante is often said to have started Italian literature, because he was the first important poet to write in that language (writers before him used Latin) and his poem was imitated by many later poets. Dante also developed a form of poetry used by later poets.

Dante was born in Florence, Italy. He probably studied philosophy and religion.

▼ The poet Dante, with the city of Florence behind him. The imaginary landscape also contains scenes from his greatest poem, the *Divine Comedy*.

He became a politician, but when his opponents took power, he was exiled in 1302. He traveled from place to place, and spent his last years in the Italian city of Ravenna.

The *Divine Comedy* is the make-believe story of Dante's trip through Hell, Purgatory, and Paradise. He meets many famous people from history, from mythology, and from his own time. Virgil, the famous Roman poet, takes him through Hell and Purgatory. A beautiful woman, Beatrice, guides him through Paradise, where he searches for God. The Beatrice of the poem was Beatrice Portinari, who lived in Florence. Dante saw Beatrice only twice, once when he was 9 and again when he was 18, but he remembered her all his life and thought of her as a saint. She was his inspiration for the *Divine Comedy*. The love poems of his other very famous work, *The New Life*, also are addressed to her.

▶ ▶ ▶ ▶ **FIND OUT MORE** ◀ ◀ ◀ ◀

Poetry; Virgil

DANUBE RIVER

The lilting melody of the famous "Blue Danube Waltz" was inspired by one of the great rivers of the world. The Danube River rises in the Black Forest in southwestern Germany and flows 1,750 miles (2,818 km) eastward to the Black Sea. It touches the countries of Germany, Austria, Slovakia, Hungary, Croatia, Bosnia and Herzegovina, Yugoslavia, Bulgaria, and Romania. The river forms the border between several of these countries. The capitals of three countries lie along the banks of the Danube—Vienna, Austria; Budapest, Hungary; and Belgrade, Yugoslavia. (See the map with the article on EUROPE.)

The Danube is the second longest river in Europe (only the Volga River is longer). It has always been an avenue of migration, conquest, and trade. It is still a busy river today. Tugs tow large barges carrying coal, oil, and iron ore. If you were a crewman on such a barge, a tug might tow you from the Black Sea upstream to Regensburg, Germany—a journey of 1,200 miles (1,932 km). Early in your journey, you would pass through a narrow gorge called the Iron Gate, where Romania and Yugoslavia built a large hydroelectric power plant. You would see many sights, such as farmers cultivating vineyards in Yugoslavia; the city of Budapest—split into two parts, Buda and Pest, by the river; and great castles along the river in Austria.

The Danube carries a great deal of silt (mud) in its waters. Over 80 million tons of silt are deposited in the Danube's delta every year. Constant dredging is needed to keep the river navigable, but still the Danube's delta is growing into the Black Sea by 80 to 100 feet (24 to 30 m) each year.

DARK MATTER

Dark matter is an invisible substance that makes up about nine-tenths of all the mass in the universe. It is called "dark" because scientists have not detected any light or other *radiation* coming from it.

Normally, astronomers can learn a great deal about objects by studying the light coming from them. They can tell an object's *mass* (overall quantity) and the speed at which it is traveling away from the Earth.

In the 1970s, astronomers noticed something strange while observing *galaxies* (distant groups of millions of stars). The light emitted from these galaxies suggested that they had a certain mass. But they were traveling at speeds that meant that they had ten times more mass. The *gravitational force* of some sort of unseen matter must have accounted for the difference.

Scientists remain uncertain about how to explain this "dark matter," or "missing matter" as it is sometimes called. Maybe it is made up of small, dense objects that are too small to shine like stars. Another theory suggests that it consists of mysterious objects called *WIMPs* (weakly interacting massive particles).

▶▶▶▶ **FIND OUT MORE** ◀◀◀◀
Astronomy; Gravity and Gravitation; Universe

DARTS

Darts is an old English game that has become popular in many countries, especially the United States. The game is played by throwing darts, small arrows each with a sharp metal point and guiding feathers at the other end. They are thrown at a board, usually made of cork or bristle. The dart board is divided into 20 segments, like the slices of a cake. Each segment has a different number.

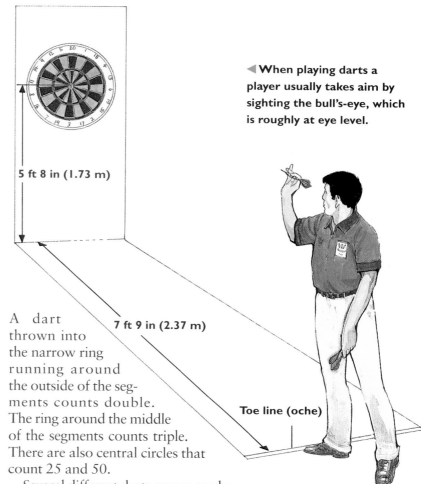

5 ft 8 in (1.73 m)

7 ft 9 in (2.37 m)

Toe line (oche)

A dart thrown into the narrow ring running around the outside of the segments counts double. The ring around the middle of the segments counts triple. There are also central circles that count 25 and 50.

Several different darts games can be played, but the most popular is that in which each player starts with 301 and reduces it to zero by subtracting each score as he or she throws. Each player takes alternate turns with three darts and must begin and end his score with a double.

There are now many international darts tournaments.

▶▶▶▶ **FIND OUT MORE** ◀◀◀◀
Games

DARWIN, CHARLES (1809–1882)

Charles Darwin wrote a book, *On the Origin of Species,* first published in England in 1859. Darwin's ideas brought about a revolution in the science of biology, in how we think of ourselves, and in our ideas about the history of Earth.

◀ **When playing darts a player usually takes aim by sighting the bull's-eye, which is roughly at eye level.**

▼ **Dart boards are usually made of cork, bristle, or elm wood.**

Berry-feeding **Seed-feeding**

Cactus-feeding **Insect-feeding**

▲ **Heads of finches from different islands in the Galápagos. Darwin hit upon his *theory of evolution by natural selection* when he saw these minor differences.**

▲ **Charles Darwin, who with Alfred Russel Wallace, created the theory of evolution by natural selection.**

▼ **H.M.S. *Beagle*, the ship in which Darwin set sail for South America and the Pacific, at anchor in the Galápagos Islands.**

Many people of Darwin's time thought that Earth—and all forms of life on it—were created less than 6,000 years ago. They thought each *species* (kind) of animal and plant was created exactly as they knew it. Some scientists did not accept this belief. They thought that plants and animals had slowly changed and developed, or evolved, over thousands of years. But they had no proof for their ideas.

Darwin was born in Shrewsbury, England. He went to Edinburgh and Cambridge universities. His father wanted him to be a minister, but Darwin was more interested in studying nature. When he was 22, Darwin became the naturalist on the five-year voyage of the H.M.S. *Beagle*. As the ship explored the Pacific Ocean, Darwin discovered a peculiar fact. Although the finches of the Galápagos Islands (off the coast of Ecuador) were much like other finches, they differed in several small ways. What could this mean?

Darwin returned to London in 1836. He puzzled over the problem of the different finches, and other questions, for 20 years. His answers to these questions, published in *On the Origin of Species*, caused violent debate because he attacked the general and religious beliefs of so many people.

Darwin published *The Descent of Man* in 1871. This new book made the argument even more bitter,

because Darwin claimed that human beings have the same ancestors as chimpanzees and other apes. Many people of Darwin's time were furious because they believed that humankind was not related to any other animal, but was specially created by God. Today, most scientists generally accept Darwin's theory.

▶▶▶▶ **FIND OUT MORE** ◀◀◀◀
Evolution; Genetics; Plant Breeding; Protective Coloring; Wallace, Alfred Russell

◼ DATA PROTECTION

Businesses and government agencies store a great deal of information on computers, in what are known as *data bases*. Most of this information is private. But many of these data bases can be accessed by unscrupulous computer operators, known as *hackers*. They find ways of breaking into these data bases and gaining access to the information.

A great deal of government information is of value to a state's enemies. A company's secrets are of interest to business rivals. So to protect data, Congress has passed a law making it a criminal offense to gain access to Federal government or business computers without authorization. Several states recognize information stored in computer data bases as property and liable to the laws governing theft.

▶▶▶▶ **FIND OUT MORE** ◀◀◀◀
Computer

DAVIS FAMILY

Father and son, Benjamin Oliver Davis and Benjamin Oliver Davis Jr., were both distinguished military men.

Benjamin Davis senior was born in Washington, D.C. He fought as a volunteer first lieutenant in the Spanish-American War in 1898. He enlisted as a private after the war. He won a competitive examination and became the first black officer in the Regular Army in 1901. Davis then became the Army's first black general in 1940. He retired in 1948.

Benjamin Oliver Davis Jr. decided early in life to become a military officer like his father before him. In high school he was a top student, a fine athlete, and president of his class.

He won an appointment to West Point Military Academy in 1932. He was the only black in a class of 383 cadets. No black had graduated from West Point in 50 years. His fellow cadets practically ignored him for four years. But he refused to quit, and he graduated with honors in 1936.

Lieutenant Davis became a pilot shortly after graduation and led the first fighter group of black pilots—the "Tuskegee Group"—during World War II. He held the rank of lieutenant general—the second highest rank in the U.S. military—when he retired in 1970. He earned 39 medals for heroism and outstanding service to his country.

▶ ▶ ▶ ▶ **FIND OUT MORE** ◀ ◀ ◀ ◀
Army; Air Force

DAVIS, JEFFERSON (1808–1889)

When the Southern states *seceded* (broke away) from the Union to form the Confederacy, they chose Jefferson Davis as their president. Davis is one of history's "unknown" men. Most accounts of the Civil War tell very little about him.

Jefferson Davis was born in Fairview, Kentucky, not far from the birthplace of Abraham Lincoln. His father was a veteran of the Revolutionary War. Davis's family moved to Mississippi soon after he was born. He attended West Point Military Academy. Lieutenant Davis fought in the Black Hawk Indian war in 1832. He then resigned from the army and married Sarah Taylor, the daughter of Zachary Taylor (who later served as twelfth U.S. president). Sarah died three months after the marriage, and Davis devoted all his time to his plantation. He organized a model democracy for the 30 slaves he owned.

Davis was elected a U.S. representative in 1845. He also married Varina Howell, daughter of a rich planter, in that year. He then fought as a colonel in the Mexican War. He served as a senator and as secretary of war under President Franklin Pierce.

Davis returned to the Senate in 1857. Arguments about slavery grew more heated, and Davis spoke more and more strongly for slavery and for states' rights. He sincerely believed that slavery was necessary in the South, and that the whole South would collapse if slavery were stopped too quickly. He also believed that slaves had to learn to be citizens and that they were not ready to be free.

Mississippi seceded from the Union in December 1860, and Davis resigned from the Senate. In February 1861, the Confederate convention chose him as president. Davis's leadership of the Southern states was often criticized by other Southerners who believed that he did not raise enough money to fight the war or that he made poor military decisions. But Davis was able to make the Confederacy strong enough to withstand the Union—which had more men, materials, and money—for four years.

After the war, Davis was charged with treason. He was imprisoned for two years but was released without trial. While in prison, he gained the

▲ **Benjamin Oliver Davis, Sr., the first black general in the U.S. Army.**

▼ **Benjamin Oliver Davis Jr., the first black general in the U.S. Air Force.**

▲ **Jefferson Davis, president of the Confederacy during the Civil War. His birthday is a public holiday in the South.**

respect of many people, from both North and South. After his release, he returned to Mississippi, where he spent the rest of his life. His book, *The Rise and Fall of the Confederate Government*, recounts his experiences.

▶▶▶▶ **FIND OUT MORE** ◀◀◀◀
Civil War; Confederate States of America; Indian Wars; Mexican War; Slavery

LEARN BY DOING

To see how night and day happen, get a rubber ball, a knitting needle, and a flashlight (or you can use a globe as in the illustration). Stick the knitting needle through the middle of the ball and mark an X on one side of the ball with ink. Imagine that the ball is the Earth. The needle is the Earth's axis. The flashlight is the sun. Shine the flashlight on the ball. The front of the ball is lighted (day). The back of the ball is dark (night). The sides get just a little light (dawn or twilight). Now turn the needle slowly, so that the ball turns. The X moves through the light and back into the dark. Imagine that the X on the ball is the place where you live on the Earth. As the Earth spins, you move from the dark to the sunlight and day begins. During the day, you move through the sunlight. When you have spun away from the sun, night begins again.

▼ **The amount of daylight plants receive affects how they grow and flower.**

SHORT DAY PLANT

Chrysanthemum

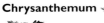

Grown during long days   **Grown during short days**

LONG DAY PLANT

Petunia

Grown during long days   **Grown during short days**

DAVY, SIR HUMPHRY

SEE ELEMENT

DAY AND NIGHT

People once believed that day and night happened because the sun moved around the Earth. Today we know this is not true. Day and night occur because the Earth is turning, spinning like a huge top. It turns around its axis. The two ends of the Earth's axis are the North and South poles. The Earth makes one complete spin every 24 hours. As it turns, half of the Earth faces toward the sun. There it is day. On the other half of the Earth, facing away from the sun, it is night.

The axis of the Earth is tilted slightly. The North Pole tilts toward the sun in the summer and away from the sun in the winter. This makes summer days longer and hotter and winter days shorter and colder.

▶▶▶▶ **FIND OUT MORE** ◀◀◀◀
Season; Solar System; Sun; Time

DAY OF THE WEEK

Have you ever wondered where the names for the days of the week came from? The names—and the reasons for the names—are different in different languages. In English, the names of three days—Sunday, Monday, and Saturday—come from the ancient Romans. They named all seven days after the sun, the moon, and the planets they knew. The names for the planets were also the names of their gods. Sunday was the sun's day. Monday was the moon's day. The other five days were named after Mars, Mercury, Jupiter, Venus, and Saturn in that order. Some languages, such as French, still have versions of these ancient Roman names

▼ The chief god of the Vikings was called Odin or Woden. The day of the week, Wednesday, is named after him.

for the days. In French these days are: *mardi* (Tuesday), *mercredi* (Wednesday), *jeudi* (Thursday), *vendredi* (Friday), and *samedi* (Saturday).

In English, the other four days do not have Roman names. The Anglo-Saxons, a Germanic people who settled in England about 1,500 years ago, made some changes. The Anglo-Saxons dropped the Roman names for four days and named these days after their own gods. Mars's day became Tuesday, after Tiw, their god of war. Mercury's day became Wednesday, after Woden, leader of their gods. Jupiter's day was changed to Thursday, after Thor, the god of thunder. And Venus's day became Friday, named after Frigga, Woden's wife and queen of the gods.

▶▶▶▶ **FIND OUT MORE** ◀◀◀◀
Gods and Goddesses

DEAD SEA

Imagine water in which you can't sink, even if you can't swim. Imagine water so salty that it burns your eyes and leaves white crystals on your body when it dries. That is what the water is like in the Dead Sea.

Despite its name, the Dead Sea is neither dead nor a sea. It is a lake, 1,320 feet (402 m) below sea level, located at the bottom of the deepest valley in the world. Although there is no life in its deep waters, the lake supports a few kinds of simple plants and a few fish near the shore. The Dead Sea forms part of the border between Israel and Jordan, both of which extract salt, potash, and bromine from the water.

The Jordan River flows into the Dead Sea. Like all river water, the water of the Jordan contains dissolved salts and minerals. Most other lakes have an outlet through which water can pass. When water flows out of a lake through an outlet, it carries its salts along. The Dead Sea does not have an outlet. Water can leave the Dead Sea only when it is evaporated by the sun. Evaporated water leaves its salts behind. This explains what makes the Dead Sea so salty.

Salt water has more *buoyancy* (the upward push of a liquid on an object) than fresh water. The saltier the water, the greater its buoyancy. The Dead Sea, the saltiest body of water in the world, is more buoyant than any other body of water.

▶▶▶▶ **FIND OUT MORE** ◀◀◀◀
Buoyancy; Great Salt Lake; Lake

▲ The Dead Sea, lies between Israel and Jordan.

▲ The Dead Sea is nine times as salty as an ocean. Swimmers float much higher in the Dead Sea because it is so salty.

LEARN BY DOING

Cut a piece of potato about the size of a large marble. The potato will sink in a large glass filled with water. Stir salt into the water, one teaspoonful at a time, until the potato rises and floats on the surface of the water. Next pour off half of the salty water. Add clear water slowly. What does the potato do? How does this help you to understand the Dead Sea?

▲ A portion of one of the Dead Sea Scrolls, the oldest known copies of the Old Testament.

▲ Sand dunes in Death Valley, which is known also for its unique rock formations and salt flats.

▼ Bobcats thrive in the mountainous and stony land of the Southwestern states. They are one of 26 species of mammals living in Death Valley.

DEAD SEA SCROLLS

In 1947, a Bedouin shepherd boy was looking for a lost goat in the hills near the Dead Sea, east of Jerusalem. He wandered into a cave, found some jars, and opened one. He was disappointed when all he saw were pieces of parchment and papyrus covered with writing. But to the world they marked the first discovery of the ancient writings called the Dead Sea Scrolls. Many more manuscripts were found in nearby caves in the Qumran Valley in the late 1940s and early 1950s. They had been preserved because the atmosphere of the region is so dry.

Several complete scrolls and thousands of smaller pieces were discovered. The handwritten scrolls were translated and found to be the oldest known copies of the Old Testament books of the Bible. At least sections of all of the books of the Old Testament, except *Esther,* are included in the find. They are written in ancient Hebrew and Aramaic, the language Christ spoke, and are 1,000 years older than any other known Bible texts. The scrolls were probably written between 200 B.C. and A.D. 68.

The scrolls may have been part of a library that belonged to a Jewish religious group, possibly the Essenes. In 1951 archeologists in the area dug up a *sciptorium,* a writing room, in which were tables and even inkwells. This may have been where the scrolls were written. Other bits and pieces of writings have been found, in addition to the books of the Bible.

Finding the Dead Sea Scrolls has been of great value to students of ancient people, especially to Bible scholars. Some of the Dead Sea Scrolls are on display in The Shrine of the Book, at the Israel Museum in Jerusalem. Others belong to Jordan.

► ► ► ► **FIND OUT MORE** ◄ ◄ ◄ ◄
Bible; Book

DEAF, EDUCATION OF THE

SEE SPECIAL EDUCATION

DEAFNESS

SEE HEARING

DEATH VALLEY

The hottest, driest, and lowest place in the United States is Death Valley. It lies mostly in southern California, but a small part extends into Nevada. Death Valley lies between two mountain ranges, the Panamint Range west of the valley and the Amargosa Range to the east. About 500 square miles (1,300 sq. km) of the valley are below sea level, including the lowest spot in the Western Hemisphere—282 feet (86 m) below sea level.

Around 26 species of mammals, including the coyote, kit-fox, and kangaroo rat live there as well as 14 species of birds. There are several species of lizards and even two kinds of tiny fish. A few plants grow there, including the mesquite, creosote bush, and desert holly. The desert and surrounding area make up the Death Valley National Monument.

In summer, Death Valley has temperatures that commonly reach 120°F (49°C). On July 10, 1913, the temperature there reached 134°F (56.7°C), the highest temperature ever recorded in the U.S. At night, the valley can become very cold. Less than 2 inches (5 cm) of rain fall annually in Death Valley. Many peo-

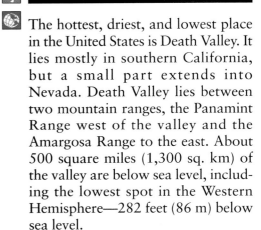

ple enjoy the warm winter sunshine of the area, which has become a popular winter-resort spot.

Death Valley was named by survivors of a group of prospectors who crossed the valley in 1849. Other names in the area are just as sinister—Funeral Mountains, Deadman Pass, Desolation Canyon, Poison Spring, and Rattlesnake Gulch.

Early prospectors came to Death Valley looking for gold, silver, lead, and borax. A few mines paid off but most produced little. Today, ghost towns stand quietly in the desert.

▶▶▶▶ **FIND OUT MORE** ◀◀◀◀
Desert

DEBS, EUGENE V. (1855–1926)

Eugene Victor Debs was one of the great pioneers of the U.S. labor movement. Born in Terre Haute, Indiana, he worked at various jobs before becoming a locomotive fireman for a railroad. He served as secretary and treasurer for the Brotherhood of Locomotive Firemen, a labor union, from 1880 to 1893. He was elected to the Indiana Legislature from 1884 to 1893. He saw a need for a union for all railroad workers, and in 1893 he organized the American Railway Union (ARU). The ARU supported a strike of Pullman-car workers the next year, and the whole union went on strike. President Cleveland sent in federal troops to break the strike. Debs was sent to prison for six months.

While in jail, he became deeply interested in the political system called *socialism*. He formed the Social Democratic Party of America in 1898. He ran for President as a socialist in 1900, 1904, 1908, 1912, and 1920. His 1920 campaign was the most successful. He ran it from prison, where he had been sent for making speeches against World War I. He was freed in 1921 after serving three years. He

won respect for his strong devotion to his beliefs, even among those who did not agree with him.

▶▶▶▶ **FIND OUT MORE** ◀◀◀◀
Labor Union; Socialism

DEBUSSY, CLAUDE (1862–1918)

A French composer rebelled against the musical traditions of his time. He was Claude Achille Debussy, who developed a new style of music, called *Impressionism*, which tried to create certain moods. His work helped shape modern music.

Debussy was born near Paris, France. An aunt encouraged him to learn piano, and he passed the entrance examinations to study at the Paris Conservatory (music school) when he was 11. When he was 22, he won a prize (*Prix de Rome*) that allowed him to study in Rome for two years.

Debussy returned to Paris and became part of a group of young French poets and painters who were seeking new ways of writing and painting. These artists influenced each other, and a poem by Symbolist poet Stephane Mallarmé inspired Debussy to compose *Prelude to the Afternoon of a Faun* for orchestra. This famous piece is a *tone poem*, a "poem" for an orchestra. It was followed by Debussy's one opera, *Pelleas and Melisande*.

Listen to Debussy's piano composition *Clair de Lune* ("Moonlight"), and you can see why his music is called impressionistic. What picture do you get from the delicate melody and the light, graceful harmony? Debussy's music uses the rhythm to create an impression on the listener, an emotion he or she would feel on a soft, moonlit evening.

▶▶▶▶ **FIND OUT MORE** ◀◀◀◀
Composer; Impressionism; Modern Music

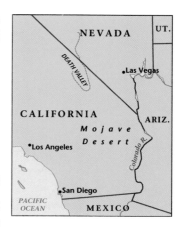

▲ **The lowest part of Death Valley is the lowest area of land in the Western Hemisphere.**

▲ **Eugene Debs, U.S. labor leader and socialist.**

SPECIAL EVENTS IN DECEMBER

2 President Monroe proclaimed the Monroe Doctrine in a message to Congress (1823).

First nuclear chain reaction produced at University of Chicago (1942).

3 First heart transplant performed in South Africa by Doctor Christiaan Barnard (1967).

Boeing 747 jumbo jetliner made its public preview flight from Seattle to New York City (1969).

President Bush and President Gorbachev announced the end of the Cold War (1989).

5 President Martin Van Buren was born (1782).

Walt Disney, creator of movies loved by children the world over, was born (1901).

Prohibition ended in the United States (1933).

6 Feast of St. Nicholas celebrated in much of Europe. The tradition of Santa Claus comes from this festival.

Calvin Coolidge broadcast the first Presidential message over radio (1923).

7 Japan attacked the United States at Pearl Harbor (1941)

8 The United States declared war on Japan (1941).

9 Joel Chandler Harris, American author of the Uncle Remus stories, was born (1848).

10 Emily Dickinson, American poet, was born (1830).

Spain ceded the Philippines to the United States (1898).

11 King Edward VIII of England abdicated his throne (1936).

Germany and Italy declared war on the United States (1941).

12 Marconi received the first radio signal sent over the Atlantic Ocean, from England to Newfoundland (1901).

13 St. Lucia's Day, festival of light. In Sweden, the eldest daughter wears a crown of lighted candles at this winter celebration.

14 President George Washington died (1799).

Roald Amundsen, explorer, arrived at South Pole (1911).

15 Royal and Ancient Society of Polar Bears General Assembly in Hammerfest, Norway. Arctic explorers meet to tell tall stories about their deeds.

Ludwig van Beethoven, German composer, was born (1770).

16 The Boston Tea Party took place. Colonists resisting the tea tax threw a shipment of tea overboard in Boston Harbor (1773).

17 Orville Wright made the first heavier-than-air flight at Kitty Hawk, North Carolina (1903).

20 France sold Louisiana territory to the United States (1803).

21 Forefather's Day, a New England holiday, honoring the landing of the Pilgrims at Plymouth in 1620.

Apollo 8 became the first manned mission to orbit the moon (1968).

23 Feast of the Radishes. (People and animals, carved out of radishes, are sold on the streets of Oaxaca, Mexico.)

24 Festival of Christmas Lanterns, a procession of colorful and gigantic lanterns in the Philippines.

25 Christmas Day, celebrating Christ's birthday.

26 St. Stephen's Day, a national holiday in England, commonly called Boxing Day (because of the tradition of giving Christmas boxes).

28 President Woodrow Wilson was born (1856).

29 President Andrew Johnson was born (1808).

31 New Year's Eve.

DECEMBER

December is the twelfth and last month of the year. It has 31 days. In Latin *decem* means "ten." December got its name because, in early Roman times, it was the tenth month. However, Julius Caesar changed the old calendar and added two new months to a new calendar. This made December the twelfth month.

▶ **December's flower is the daffodil or narcissus.**

▼ **One of December's birthstones is turquoise.**

Winter begins in December in the middle latitudes of the Northern Hemisphere. The first day of winter, December 21 or 22, is called the *winter solstice*, the shortest day of the year. In the middle latitudes of the Southern Hemisphere, summer begins at that time.

December's great holiday in many parts of the world is Christmas. Christian peoples celebrate the birth of Christ on this day, December 25. The eight-day Jewish Feast of Lights, Hanukkah, usually comes in December. The last night of the month is New Year's Eve (or Hogmanay), an evening when people stay up until midnight to welcome in the new year. December's birthstones now are the zircon and turquoise. Narcissus is the flower of the month. The holly, poinsettia, and mistletoe, used for Christmas decorations, are also associated with December.

▶▶▶▶ **FIND OUT MORE** ◀◀◀◀
Caesar, Julius; Calendar; Christmas; Hanukkah; Holiday; Month; New Year's Day; Season; Winter

DECIDUOUS TREE

SEE TREE

DECIMAL NUMBER

The number system we use is called the *decimal* number system. The word "decimal" comes from the Latin word for "ten." Our number system is based on ten and other numbers produced by multiplying ten by itself several times, such as 100, 1,000, 10,000.

We have only ten symbols for whole numbers: 1, 2, 3, 4, 5, 6, 7, 8, 9, and 0. These symbols are called *numerals*. Depending on their place in a number they can stand for groups of ones, tens, hundreds, thousands, and so on. In this way we can tell that the number 1,259 means 1 group of 1,000, plus 2 groups of 100, plus 5 groups of 10, plus 9 units.

Fractions in the decimal system are called *decimal fractions*. (See the box on fractions in this article. Be sure you understand what "numerator" and "denominator" mean.) A decimal fraction is one whose denominator is 10, 100, 1,000, and so forth. A decimal point is used to show what number is in the denominator.

The following are all decimal numbers that are part fractions and part whole numbers. The decimal points are in red:
12.3 1.17 46.395
The number to the left of the decimal point is a whole number. The number to the right of the decimal

---

DECIMAL FRACTIONS

Decimal fractions can be made from ordinary fractions by dividing the denominator into the numerator. A decimal fraction can be thought of as a fraction of 10. For example $\frac{1}{2}$ is the same as $\frac{5}{10}$ or 0.5.

A fraction $\frac{1}{2}$ — Numerator / Denominator

A decimal fraction **0.5**

$$\mathbf{1/8 = 1 \div 8 = 0.125}$$

---

point is a fraction. To form the fraction, place the entire number to the right of the decimal point in the numerator. In the denominator, put a 1 with as many zeros (0s) after it as there are numbers to the right of the decimal point. For example:

$$0.3 = \frac{3}{10}$$
$$0.17 = \frac{17}{100}$$
$$0.395 = \frac{395}{1,000}$$

The entire decimal number is the whole number to the left of the decimal point *plus* the fraction to the right of the decimal point. For example:
12.3 = 12 + 3/10 = 12 and three-tenths
1.17 = 1 + 17/100 = one and 17 one-hundredths
46.395 = 46 + 395/1,000 = 46 and 395 one-thousandths
Decimal fractions are used because they are much easier to work with than ordinary fractions. They can be added, subtracted, multiplied, and divided using the same methods as for whole numbers. For this reason, many money systems and measuring systems use a decimal system. Dollars and cents are an example. The decimal number $2.43 means "two dollars and 43 one-hundredths of a dollar."

The *metric system* of measuring is a decimal system now used by most countries.

▶▶▶▶ **FIND OUT MORE** ◀◀◀◀
Measurement; Metric System; Number

▼ **The decimal, or metric, system of measuring is used by most countries. This brass prototype weighs the original standard kilogram.**

It has been said that the most important invention of all time was the invention of the decimal number system. The man who invented the system was a Dutch mathematician born 400 years ago. His name was Simon Stevin or Stevinus. His great idea was that the decimal point numbers before the point should be whole numbers, those after it should be fractions.

DECLARATION OF INDEPENDENCE

"All men are created equal." So states the Declaration of Independence, written in 1776. This historic document declared the 13 American colonies free from British rule.

For more than ten years friction had been building between the American colonies and Britain. In May 1775, delegates from all the colonies met in Philadelphia at the Second Continental Congress to discuss their grievances with the unfairness of British rule.

Some delegates hoped to come to an agreement with Britain without war. Other delegates argued that Americans would never have their full rights unless they declared their independence. One delegate, Richard Henry Lee of Virginia, introduced a declaration in June 1776, stating that

▼ The Declaration of Independence, signed by patriots in Independence Hall, Philadelphia, in 1776.

the colonies "are, and of a right ought to be, free and independent states." The delegates voted for Lee's statement on July 2, 1776. Meanwhile, they asked Thomas Jefferson to write a formal declaration. John Adams, Robert Livingston, Roger Sherman, and Benjamin Franklin helped Jefferson write the final draft.

On July 4, 1776, delegates from 12 colonies formally accepted Jefferson's draft of the Declaration of Independence (New York temporarily abstained). Fifty-six delegates from all 13 colonies signed it on August 2, 1776. News of the adoption of the Declaration soon spread.

The Declaration has two main parts. One paragraph tells of the rights of all people. It says that God creates all men equal. All persons have certain rights that no government can take away. Among these rights are the right to live, to be free, and to do those things that make him happy, so long as no one is harmed. Every person, no matter who he or she is, should be treated as a human being. Government must be set up to protect these rights. The people have a right to change a government if it does not serve them. The second part of the Declaration explains how the British king had taken away the colonists' rights. The document ends with a declaration that the colonies are free from the king's rule.

This historic document has aroused people in other countries to make their governments more democratic. Many countries have been made independent since it was signed. The original parchment copy of the Declaration of Independence is displayed with the U.S. Constitution in the National Archives building in Washington, D.C.

▶▶▶▶ **FIND OUT MORE** ◀◀◀◀

Adams, John; American Colonies; Continental Congress; Franklin, Benjamin; Jefferson, Thomas; Revolutionary War

DEEP-SEA LIFE

The deeper you go in the sea the darker it gets. In the deepest parts of the ocean, below about 3,300 feet (1,000 m), it is completely dark and many of the fishes and other animals have their own internal lights. These lights help the animals to find food and to recognize their mates.

There are no plants in the depths. The animals are all either flesh eaters or scavengers feeding on the debris sinking down from higher levels. Very little food actually gets down to the deepest parts and not a lot of animals can live there. Those that do manage to survive are all rather small, but they include some formidable predators. Most of the fishes have enormous mouths compared with the rest of the body. They don't find food very often and they must be able to tackle anything they meet—even if it is as large or even larger than themselves. Many also have jaws full of needlelike teeth, which ensure that the prey never escapes. For example, *gulpers* appear to be little more than a mouth with a long tail. The tail has a *luminous* (lighted) lure at the end, and when a victim approaches the "bait" it is lassoed by the whiplike tail. *Angler-fishes* commonly have luminous lures hanging just above their enormous mouths. *Pachystomius*, a slender fish living just above the level of total darkness, uses a red searchlight to pick out its prey. The light streams out from near its eyes and, as most other fishes cannot see red light, the predator can approach them unseen.

Other creatures of the deep sea world include various prawns and numerous squids. The latter are often beautifully colored and carry lots of luminous spots.

▶▶▶▶ **FIND OUT MORE** ◀◀◀◀
Bioluminescence

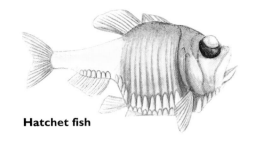

Hatchet fish

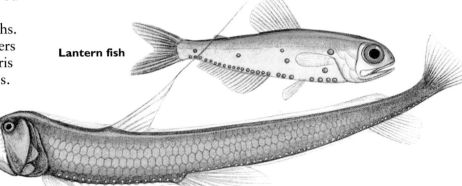

Lantern fish

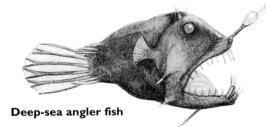

Viper fish

Deep-sea angler fish

◀ Some forms of deep-sea fishes can be very strange indeed! Many have organs that light up to attract prey.

DEER

Deer make up one of the best known mammal families. They are native to North and South America, Europe, Asia, and Africa and have been introduced to the islands of Hawaii, Australia, and New Zealand.

Deer belong to the mammal group *ungulates* (hoofed mammals). They range in size from about 20 pounds (9 kg) to more than 1,800 pounds (816 kg). They live in cold regions, in hot regions, in forests, on grassy plains, on deserts, on mountains, and on flat plateaus. But they all have certain features in common. They are all *herbivores* (plant eaters), and they all feed by browsing, or grazing. They eat leaves, twigs, bark, grasses, and

▼ The sika deer, a native of eastern Asia that has been introduced to Europe.

▲ Deer antlers grow each year from tender stumps. The four stages pictured here show the period from spring to fall. To begin with, the antlers are covered in a layer of soft, hair-covered skin called *velvet*. When the antlers are fully grown the velvet is rubbed off.

▼ Deer of North America. Male deer use their antlers mainly for fighting one another.

Moose

Mule Deer

Woodland caribou

White-tailed deer

Wapiti (elk)

lichens. They also eat buds, berries, and other fruit.

The male of most species is called a *buck* and the female a *doe*. The male red deer of Europe and Asia may be called a *stag* or a *hart* and the female deer may be called a *hind*. A male moose or caribou is a *bull,* and a female a *cow*. Most young deer are called *fawns,* but a baby wapiti, moose, or caribou is a *calf*.

Deer are the only animals with antlers. Males of almost all species have them, and so do female caribou and reindeer. Antlers are made of bone. They grow from two bony bumps, called *pedicles*, on the forehead. Antlers are shed and replaced every year.

Kinds of Deer

Whitetail deer, or Virginia deer, are found in greater numbers and in more places than other deer. They live in forests from the East Coast to the Rocky Mountains, and from southern Canada to northern South America. The deer browse on many kinds of grasses, weeds, shrubs, twigs, fungi, nuts, and lichens.

A whitetail doe often gives birth to twin fawns in spring or summer. A tiny fawn has a light-brown coat spotted with white patches. This coloring looks very much like patches of sunlight on the forest floor, and helps the fawn to hide from its enemies. The fawn grows so quickly that it is almost the size of its mother by fall. Its coat slowly changes to the heavy, gray-brown winter coat. The next summer, the young deer will have a coat of light reddish brown. A full-grown whitetail weighs 50 to 300 pounds (23–135 kg).

The *mule deer* is the whitetail's close relative. Mule deer are found from the Great Plains to the west coast of North America, from Canada to Mexico. They have large eyes, exceptionally big ears (from which they get their name), and rounded white tails tipped with black.

The North American *blacktail* is smaller than the mule deer, and its ears are short and broad. Lewis and Clark, the famous explorers, were the first white men to see this deer, and they gave it its misleading name. Blacktails' tails are bushy and black, but the undersides are bright white. Blacktails range from around San Diego, California, to Sitka, Alaska.

The largest member of the deer family is the *Alaska moose*. Bulls weigh 1,800 pounds (816 kg) or more and have an antler spread of over 6 feet (1.8 m). Cows are smaller. One to three calves are born in late spring.

Moose are found in only 12 states. Hunters killed so many that they have almost disappeared. Moose are protected by law in the United States and Canada. Moose also live in the northern forests of Europe and Asia, where they are called *elk*.

The *wapiti*, or *American elk*, once lived from the eastern forests to the west coast of North America. But as settlers spread across the country, the elk quickly died out. By the late 1800s, elk were plentiful only in Yellowstone National Park. Then, around 1900, men from the National Park Service, part of the U.S. Department of the Interior, began to trap small groups of elk from the Yellowstone herds. The captured elk were given to state game departments to restore elk to their former homes. Elk herds live in 39 states today.

Caribou live in Alaska and Canada on tundras and spruce forests. Herds travel great distances in search of slow-growing lichen on which they feed. Unlike other female deer, caribou cows have antlers. Bulls shed their large, many branched antlers during November and December. Cows and young bulls shed their much smaller horns in May or June.

The caribou's first cousin is the European and Asian *reindeer*. Reindeer are slightly smaller than caribou, and they are the only deer that have been domesticated. The Lapps and other northern Europeans keep herds for meat, milk, and clothing. They are used to pull sleds.

The world's smallest deer is the *pudu* of Chile and Bolivia. Full-grown males are only 15 inches (38 cm) tall and weigh 20 pounds (9 kg). The *Chinese water deer* is also 20 pounds (9 kg) full-grown, with curved tusks.

▶▶▶▶ **FIND OUT MORE** ◀◀◀◀
Antelope; Arctic; Hoofed Animals;
Horns and Antlers; Lewis and Clark
Expedition; Tundra

DEFENSE

SEE AIR FORCE; ARMY; MARINE CORPS; NAVY

DEFOE, DANIEL (1660–1731)

Daniel Defoe, an English writer, created the popular story of *Robinson Crusoe* in 1719. The novel tells the story of a shipwrecked sailor who builds himself a home, raises goats, and wins a trusted friend named Friday. This exciting tale is based on the life of Alexander Selkirk (1676–1721), a Scottish sailor marooned on a Pacific island for over four years.

Defoe was born in London, England. His father was a butcher named Foe. Daniel added "De" to his name to make it more fashionable. He wrote mostly about politics and religion, which sometimes got him into trouble. He spent some time in prison. Defoe then became a newspaper writer. He also acted as a secret agent for people who were trying to bring Scotland and England together.

Defoe wrote more than 500 books. *Moll Flanders* (1722), another famous Defoe book, tells the adventures of a misguided young lady who is determined to get ahead in the world. Many people think *A Journal of the Plague Year* (1722) is Defoe's best book. The disease called "bubonic plague" struck London in 1665, killing more than 70,000 people. Defoe's book pretends to be the diary of a man living in London at the time. All of these books show why Defoe is thought to be the first great realistic novelist in English fiction.

▶▶▶▶ **FIND OUT MORE** ◀◀◀◀
Novel

DE FOREST, LEE

SEE RADIO BROADCASTING

▲ **Daniel Defoe, English author, businessman, pamphleteer and newspaper proprietor.**

▲ **One of Defoe's most famous books is *Robinson Crusoe*, the story of a shipwrecked sailor.**

▼ Edgar Degas, the great French painter of ballet scenes. This sketch was done by another famous French artist, Edouard Manet.

DEGAS, EDGAR (1834–1917)

As you look at the painting of the prima ballerina dancing in her white costume, can't you almost hear the applause of the audience? Like a fairy queen she floats across the stage, while other members of the ballet company watch from backstage as she performs. Wouldn't you like to be in the audience?

The painter of *Prima Ballerina* was Edgar Degas, the greatest of all painters of the dance. He was born in Paris to wealthy parents, and grew up enjoying the arts. Unlike most artists, he came from a family that had no objection to his becoming an artist. They furnished a studio for him when he decided, at 18, that he wanted to paint. As a native Parisian, he was right at the heart of things when that city became more and

more an art center of the 1800s. He was one of the circle of painters called the *Impressionists*, who created a stir in art circles with their way of painting an impression of a scene in changing light and shade.

He first began to paint theatrical scenes in the 1860s. He painted cafe singers, circus artists, and horse races. But mostly he painted ballet dancers at rehearsal, in the dressing room, on stage, practicing at the bar. He liked to paint from unusual angles, as in the picture here. He was interested in photography and his paintings have an unposed appearance. Note the lack of detail in the dancer's face, as if she were moving. You are allowed only a fleeting glimpse of her.

Although he painted dozens of people, Degas did not get along with others and lived alone. He became more and more interested in sculpture as he got older, perhaps because his eyesight was getting worse and he could no longer see to paint.

▶▶▶▶ **FIND OUT MORE** ◀◀◀◀
Cassatt, Mary; Impressionism

▲ Degas' *Young Dancer.* Many of Degas's paintings were produced using models to study body movement.

▶ *Prima Ballerina*, a painting by Edgar Degas.

DE GAULLE, CHARLES (1890–1970)

Charles André Joseph Marie de Gaulle was the best-known French soldier and leader from 1940 to 1969. He gave France, a defeated nation in 1940, new pride. He led that country back to a leading position among Europe's nations.

De Gaulle was born near Lille, France. He graduated with honors in 1911 from St. Cyr, the famous French military school. During World War I he was wounded four times and captured by the Germans. He was a strong believer in mechanized warfare in the 1930s. During World War II, when France surrendered to Germany on June 22, 1940, de Gaulle, then a general, escaped to London, England. He refused to accept the surrender, saying that France had lost a battle, not a war. From his base in England he led and inspired the Free French army of patriots.

After the war, de Gaulle headed the French government. But he resigned in January 1946, because he felt his country's new constitution did not give him enough power. He was called back from retirement to become the French President in 1958 to deal with the crisis in Algeria. De Gaulle began a number of programs, such as increasing taxes and modernizing industry, to make France a power in the modern world and to restore what he called France's *gloire* ("glory"). He signed a treaty with an old enemy, Germany, in January 1963. He was a strong opponent of Britain's membership in the European Economic Community. When his plans for changing the French constitution were defeated in April 1969, after a referendum, he resigned. Today, French politics are still very much influenced by the ideas of de Gaulle.

▶▶▶▶ **FIND OUT MORE** ◀◀◀◀
French History; World War II

DELAWARE

Lord De La Warr was governor of the colony of Virginia in its early years, but his name, spelled differently, was given to the state of Delaware.

In the summer of 1610, Captain Samuel Argall sailed north from Virginia along the Atlantic Coast. Over 100 miles up the coast, he came to a bay. On the northern side was a cape, a point of land. He named it for the governor of his colony. (The cape, which is now in New Jersey, was renamed Cape May.) De La Warr's name, respelled Delaware, was later used for the bay, too. His name was then given to the long river that pours into the bay. The land west of the lower river and the bay also came to be called Delaware. That land became the state of Delaware.

The Land
The only state smaller than Delaware is Rhode Island. Delaware has few natural resources, but the state has one great advantage. It has a fine location. Delaware lies between the North and the South. Delaware is as far north as parts of Pennsylvania and New Jersey. It is as far south as parts of Maryland and Virginia. Delaware lies close to some of the largest industrial cities in the United States including New York, Philadelphia, Baltimore, and Washington, D.C.

The state has good water transportation. Oceangoing ships sail up the Delaware River to Wilmington. The river is connected with the Chesapeake Bay by the Chesapeake and Delaware Canal. This canal cuts through the northern end of a long *peninsula* (an "arm" of land that is almost surrounded by water). This is known as the Delmarva Peninsula because of the three states with land on it: Delaware, Maryland, and Virginia. West of the peninsula is the Chesapeake Bay. East of it are the lower Delaware River, the Delaware Bay, and the Atlantic Ocean.

The peninsula is part of the Atlantic Coastal Plain. Most of Delaware, therefore, is in the plain. For this reason, most of Delaware is low and rather flat. Some parts have so little slope that water does not drain well from them, and these parts are often swampy. The northernmost part of Delaware is not in the coastal plain. It is in a hilly region called the

▲ Charles de Gaulle, the great French general and statesman. He led the Free French opposition to the German occupation of France during World War II. Later he became French president.

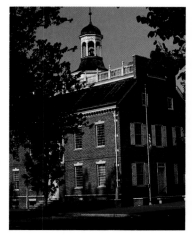
▲ The Old State House, Dover. Built in 1792, it remained Delaware's capitol building until 1933.

▲ **The Grand Opera House, Wilmington, Delaware.**

In 1800, Delaware's population was 64,000. By 1900 it had risen to 185,000. By the 1990 census the figure had risen to 666,168.

▲ **The Delaware Memorial Bridge is a superbly graceful piece of modern architecture.**

Piedmont which stretches from New Jersey to Alabama.

Delaware in winter seems just the in-between state that it is. It is not as cold as New England, to the north. But it is colder than the Deep South. The Delaware summer is hot and humid. People flock to the beaches, where ocean winds bring relief from the heat.

History

Three European flags have flown in Delaware. The Dutch flag came first. It flew from the ship Half Moon. Its captain, Henry Hudson, was English but had been hired by the Dutch. Hudson sailed into Delaware Bay in 1609, the year before Samuel Argall reached it. The Dutch built a settlement at the entrance to the bay in 1631. It stood where the fishing port of Lewes is now. The settlement was named *Swaanedael* or "Place of Swans." (The swans were probably wild geese.) The Native Americans here got along well with the Dutch at first. But a quarrel led to bloodshed, and the Native Americans killed almost everyone in the settlement.

Swedes and Finns were the first Europeans to build a lasting settlement in Delaware. Peter Minuit brought them from Europe in 1638. He was Dutch, but he was serving the 12-year-old Swedish queen, Christina. Minuit's two ships sailed up the Delaware River to the place where Wilmington stands today. There the settlers built a log fort. They named it Fort Christina. Soldiers from the Dutch colony of New Netherland captured Fort Christina and the Swedish settlement in 1655. But the victory did the Dutch little good. Less than ten years later the English seized New Netherland and renamed it New York. At the same time, the English took the Delaware territory from the Dutch.

Most of the Atlantic coast was then English, but the English colonies quarreled with each other about their boundaries. Pirates often sailed into Delaware Bay and raided towns along the shore. But in spite of such troubles, the Delaware colonists did well. Farmers raised good crops. Merchants grew rich through trade.

In 1776, Delaware became one of the 13 original United States. With its sister states, it fought Great Britain during the Revolutionary War. The First Delaware Regiment took as its nickname the "Blue Hen's Chickens." Rooster fighting was a sport in those days. And people believed that the bravest fighting roosters were those hatched from the eggs of blue hens. Sometimes Delaware is called the "Blue Hen State." Delaware is also called "The First State," because it was the first state to accept the new Constitution in 1787.

Working in Delaware

Manufacturing is Delaware's biggest business. The chemical industry is the most profitable. Canning and other methods of food preparation come next. Most factories are in and around Wilmington, Delaware's largest city. Soon after 1800, mills for weaving cloth were opened in this area. So was the state's first gunpowder mill. It was started by Eleuthère Irénée du Pont de Nemours, who had fled from France during the French Revolution. The company he founded is known today as E. I. du Pont de Nemours and Company, or Du Pont. It is a huge company, with factories in many parts of the United States. It makes chemicals, dyes, paints, rubber, and synthetic fabrics, as well as explosives. Some buildings of the early powder mill are not far away on Brandywine Creek.

Delaware agriculture earns much less money than manufacturing. But it is important. Chickens, corn, and soybeans are the principal products.

Delaware's low business taxes have attracted many corporations, which now have head offices in the state.

DECEMBER 7, 1787

STATE SYMBOLS

◄ The blue hen chicken is Delaware's state bird. It is known as a fierce fighter.

► The American holly is the state tree. It is one of Delaware's most important forest trees.

◄ The state seal shows the kinds of work important in Delaware's early history. Most men were farmers or soldiers.

► Peach blossom was adopted as Delaware's state flower in 1985.

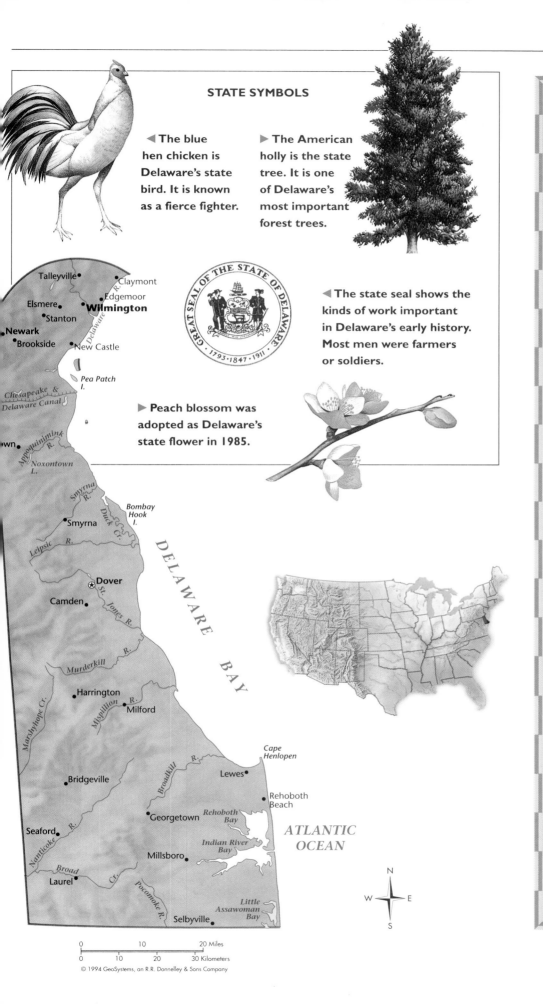

GREAT SEAL OF THE STATE OF DELAWARE · 1793·1847·1911

Talleyville
Claymont
Elsmere
Edgemoor
Stanton
Wilmington
Newark
Brookside
New Castle

Delaware R.

Pea Patch I.

Chesapeake & Delaware Canal

wn
Appoquinimink R.
Noxontown L.

Smyrna R.
Smyrna
Duck Cr.
Bombay Hook I.
Leipsic R.

Dover
St. Jones R.
Camden

Murderkill R.

Harrington
Mispillion R.
Milford

Marshyhope Cr.

Bridgeville
Broadkill R.
Cape Henlopen
Lewes
Rehoboth Beach

Seaford
Nanticoke R.
Georgetown
Rehoboth Bay
Indian River Bay
Millsboro

Broad Cr.
Laurel
Pocomoke R.
Little Assawoman Bay
Selbyville

DELAWARE BAY

ATLANTIC OCEAN

N W E S

0   10   20 Miles
0 10 20 30 Kilometers

DELAWARE

Capital
Dover (27,630 people)

Area
2,157 square miles (5,377 sq. km)
Rank: 49th

Population
666,168 people
Rank: 46th

Statehood
December 7, 1787 (First of the 13 original states to ratify the Constitution)

Principal river
Delaware (390 miles/ 628 km)

Highest point
442 feet (135 m), near Centerville, New Castle County

Largest city
Wilmington (71,520 people)

Motto
"Liberty and Independence"

Song
"Our Delaware"

Famous people
Valerie Bertinelli, Pierre Samuel du Pont

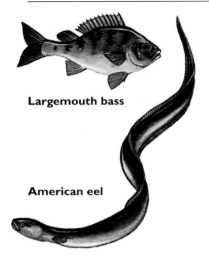

Largemouth bass

American eel

▲ Commercial fishing brings in over $4 million a year for Delaware's economy. Menhaden (a type of herring), bass, carp, eels, pike, and trout are found in Delaware's lakes, ponds and rivers.

▼ Political meetings in ancient Athens, Greece took place in the open air. Democracy was supposed to be government of the people, by the people, for the people. But not everyone could vote. Democracy did not apply to women, slaves, or foreigners.

Tourists bring millions of dollars to the state every year. Some people visit the beaches. Rehoboth Beach is popular with visitors from Baltimore, Philadelphia and Washington, D.C. Other people tour historic spots. One such spot in Wilmington is called the Rocks. This stone wharf on the Christina River is natural, not man-made. The Swedes and Finns landed there in 1638. The Old Swedes Church, built in 1698, is nearby. Before 1777, New Castle was the capital of Delaware. It has some beautiful old houses. Other points of interest are the Hagley Museum, with exhibits of early industries, and the Winterthur Museum, noted for its colonial furniture.

▶▶▶▶ **FIND OUT MORE** ◀◀◀◀
State Government

DELTA

SEE RIVER

DEMOCRACY

A political system in which people have the supreme voice in deciding how their government

should work is called a democracy. In modern democracies citizens *elect*, or choose by the process of voting, certain people to represent them. In some democratic countries, a head of government is also elected. U.S. citizens elect a President and Vice President, as well as senators and representatives who are members of Congress. They often vote for leaders of state and local governments, too. The government, which is made up of elected representatives, must carry out the wishes of the people when taking action or making laws.

Democracy comes from a Greek word meaning "rule of the people." Democracies existed in Greece and Rome, but they were different from democracies today. They were *direct* democracies in which all *citizens* could speak and vote on all the issues. But the word "citizen" only applied to men who owned property; no one else could vote. Democracies have changed, mostly because modern democracies are much larger. Can you imagine a meeting of all the citizens of the United States? Or how long it would take for everyone to suggest ideas about a new law? The United States is an *indirect* democracy or a *republic*. Citizens choose representatives who run the government.

Another change has taken place, too. Laws have been passed to protect the rights of many citizens. Now all citizens (other than children), regardless of their race, sex, or religious beliefs can vote. People living in a democracy have the right of individual freedom. They can choose their own careers and run their own businesses. All citizens are equal, and laws are supposed to be enforced the same way for all people.

Many philosophers, including John Locke and Thomas Jefferson, wrote on what they thought a democracy ought to be. Some of Jefferson's ideas are included in the Declaration of Independence. It states: "...that all men are created equal, that they are endowed by their Creator with certain unalienable Rights, that among these are Life, Liberty and the pursuit of Happiness."

The Bill of Rights, the first ten amendments to the Constitution, promises other rights for all Americans such as the freedom of speech and the freedom of the press. These rights allow people to hear, read, and discuss new ideas. These rights make it possible for people to help elected representatives and leaders make their country a better place to live. These rights even protect people in the United States from a central government that has too much power.

►►►► **FIND OUT MORE** ◄◄◄◄
Bill of Rights; Declaration of Independence; Election

DENMARK

Denmark is a prosperous country, with one of the world's highest standards of living. It is famous for its butter, cheese, ham, bacon, and pastry. Its beautifully designed furniture and silverware are also well known around the world. The Danes are today a peaceful people; however, 1,000 years ago, the Danes were

▲ **The beautiful city of Copenhagen, capital of Denmark, is one of Europe's oldest seaports.**

warlike Viking sea-raiders who were feared throughout most of Europe.

Denmark is almost entirely surrounded by water. It consists of a mainland and more than 400 islands. The mainland is part of the Jutland Peninsula in northwestern Europe. (See the map with the article on EUROPE.) Most of the Danish islands are close to the mainland. But the rocky Faeroe Islands lie 800 miles (1,290 km) away in the northern part of the Atlantic Ocean, north of the British Isles. Greenland, a huge island near the North American continent, is a self-governing Danish country.

Because it is surrounded by sea, Denmark has a pleasant climate, even though it is a northern country. The average temperature in winter is about 32°F (0°C), and in summer about 60°F (15°C).

One of the largest islands close to the mainland is Zealand (*Sjaelland* in

DENMARK

Capital city
Copenhagen
(1,339,000 people)

Area
16,629 square miles
(43,069 sq. km)

Population
5,141,000 people

Government
Constitutional monarchy

Natural resources
Crude oil, natural gas, limestone, salt

Export products
Meat, meat products, fish, dairy products, metal goods, machinery, ships

Unit of money
Krone

Official language
Danish

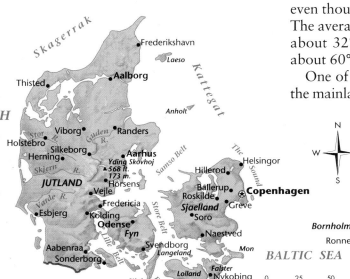

0   25   50   75   100 Miles
0 25 50 75 100 125 150 Kilometers
© 1994 GeoSystems, an R.R. Donnelley & Sons Company

▲ **The statue of the Little Mermaid sits on a rock in Copenhagen's harbor.**

Danish). It is separated from Sweden by a channel called the Oresund. Denmark's capital, Copenhagen, is on Zealand. The city was founded 800 years ago and is one of Europe's oldest seaports. It has a world-famous amusement park, called Tivoli Gardens. Another well-known landmark is the statue of the Little Mermaid in Copenhagen's harbor. It was built in honor of the Danish writer Hans Christian Andersen. You may have read his famous story about a mermaid who fell in love with a human prince.

Denmark has few natural resources. Raw materials needed by factories must be bought from other countries. But Danish soil is very fertile, and Denmark's farms are among the most prosperous in Europe. Fishing, shipping, and manufacturing are important industries.

Denmark has been a constitutional monarchy for more than 140 years. It is governed under a new constitu-tion adopted in 1953. The *monarch*, queen or king, chooses the prime minister, who is the real head of government. Queen Margrethe II, who succeeded to the throne in 1972, is only the second queen Denmark has had. The members of the one-chamber legislature are elected by the Danish people in democratic elections. The government provides insurance for illness, accidents, old age, and unemployment, but people pay very high taxes for these services. Denmark is a member of the European Community.

▶ ▶ ▶ ▶ **FIND OUT MORE** ◀ ◀ ◀ ◀

Andersen, Hans Christian; Europe; European Community; Greenland; Scandinavia; Scandinavian Languages

DENSITY

SEE BUOYANCY; MATTER

QUIZ ANSWERS

Computer quiz, page 667

1. Binary code is the system of electric code signals that a computer understands.

2. No, computers are not capable of independent thought.

3. Two kinds of computer memory units are the ROM (read-only-memory) and the RAM (random-access memory). ROM is like a person's long-term memory. RAM is like short-term memory.

4. The keyboard, mouse, joystick, light pen, and pressure-sensitive penare all input units.

5. A microchip is a tiny electronic integrated circuit. It can contain thousands of microscopic transistors that help a computer to work.

Conservation quiz, page 682

1. A conservationist is someone whose job is to find ways of protecting the environment.

2. Crop rotation is much better for the soil than one-crop farming. One-crop farming robs the ground of a lot of essential nutrients Because different crops take different food from the soil, crop rotation is a way to make sure that the soil has a chance to recover.

3. The Department of Agriculture is in charge of conservation measures in the U.S.

4. Teddy Roosevelt was the first president to establish a National Park, a protected area of land.

Continent quiz, page 694

1. The Central American countries are usually considered part of the North American continent, as they are located above the equator, in the northern hemisphere.

2. Antarctica is a continent because it is a solid land mass. The Arctic is made up of a series of islands and is not a continent.

3. In the U.S. the Continental Divide crosses north to south, following the path of the Rockies.

4. A continental shelf is the gently sloping edge of a continent, resting under the ocean. At the tip of this shelf the land suddenly drops away: this is the continental slope.

Crustacean quiz, page 728

1. Lobsters, crabs, prawns, woodlice, barnacles, and waterfleas are all common types of crustaceans.

2. A crustacean's shell is made of a tough material called *chitin*.

3. Arthropods are the largest group of animals. They include insects,centipedes and millipedes, arachnids (such as spiders) as well as crustaceans.

4. *Gooseneck* and *acorn* barnacles.

5. Both. They are at home in any cold-water environment, be it salt sea or fresh lake water.